EVIL CONJECTURES

ACCUSED OF MURDER, A NURSING HOME DOCTOR
ARGUES TO CLEAR HIS NAME

DR. STEPHEN EDWARDS

Evil Conjectures
ISBN: 978-0-6450394-4-3
Published by A Sense of Place Publishing 2022
Copyright Stephen Edwards 2022

No parts of this publication may be reproduced, stored in a retrieval system, or transmitted in any form or by any means, electronic, mechanical, photocopying, recording, or otherwise, without the prior written permission of the copyright owner.

This book is sold subject to the condition that it shall not, by way of trade or otherwise, be lent, resold, hired out, or otherwise circulated without the publisher's prior consent in any form of binding or cover other than that in which it is published and without a similar condition including this condition being imposed on the subsequent purchaser. Under no circumstances may any part of this book be photocopied for resale.

A catalogue record for this book is available from the National Library of Australia

TABLE OF CONTENTS

Prologue 7
Chapter One: The Death of David Edwards 9
Chapter Two: The Death of Nelda Edwards 13
Chapter Three: The Arrest of Stephen Edwards 21
Chapter Four: Jail Time 25
Chapter Five: Bail 55
Chapter Six: To the Coroner 69
Chapter Seven: The Experts 81
Chapter Eight: Family Conspiracy 93
Chapter Nine: Family Background 99
Chapter Ten: Preliminary Hearings 109
Chapter Eleven: The Prosecution Line-up 119
Chapter Twelve: The Medical Insurer 123
Chapter Thirteen: The Investigation 125
Chapter Fourteen: The Court Hearings 127
Epilogue 137
Appendices 145
Photographs 167
The Stories 173
Preamble 173
The look of death 175
Doris 181
The cat struck back 185
Mrs Green 187
Mr Woody 191
Phyllis 195
Local wacko 199
Matilda 203
Vera's end 205
The plateau 207
You may not find this amusing 209
The scallywag 211
The old dog 217
Spare us from the well-meaning 219
Lou: a sad tale of slow death and a last smile 223
A snippet of a story 227
Acknowledgements 229

PROLOGUE

IF YOU GOOGLE 'Dr Stephen Edwards' you will find news stories of him allegedly murdering his elderly mother, being sent to jail for three months and then on bail for four years until the case was dropped. Edwards, a former general practitioner who specialised in nursing home patients and palliative care, was deregistered after the charge of euthanising his mother was brought against him. The case was closed after he was diagnosed with terminal cancer and given six to thirteen months to live in January 2020. He left Tasmania to live in inner Sydney. The story of how Edwards was charged with conspiring with his brother to murder his mother confronts the most fundamental questions of life and death, magnified by his own diagnosis of terminal cancer which he stubbornly refuses to accept. His incarceration in Tasmania's most notorious high-security jail brought him into direct contact with mass murderer Martin Bryant as well as the inequities and perverse injustices of the prison system. Dubbed 'Dr Death' by his fellow inmates, he nevertheless earned their respect. He was only the second person in Australia to be granted bail for murder, and his treatment highlights the lottery that is the justice system. Perversely, the dropping of the charges against him makes it impossible to clear his name. His narrative of the events that led to his murder charge and his fight for justice makes for compelling reading.

CHAPTER ONE: THE DEATH OF DAVID EDWARDS

Garden Island Creek, southern Tasmania, July 2016: Gloom and the cold rain slid down my neck. Gusts of wind had reduced my umbrella to a broken thing as I stood next to a hopelessly bogged ute by a row of post boxes at a country road intersection. How has this happened to me? I asked mutely of the grey sky. Why? Locals soon stopped and commiserated on the perils of newly graded, unsealed road shoulders, while calmly applying a towrope and saving my day. Damp and mud-splattered, I arrived on time in the city for a legal meeting early on in the four-year circus of the investigation of the murder charge against me.

How had this befallen me? A dedicated and valued doctor who left family and the perpetual winter of Tasmania behind as a teenager to live in Sydney most of his life. Here I was in wet clothes driving a ute in heavy rain down dirt roads. Why me? When will this nightmare be over? Will then sun ever shine again?

Did I murder my mother? That is now for you to decide. The case against me was dismissed on medical grounds. I am now denied a formal trial by jury. Not only did the new plague of the COVID-19 virus further delay already backlogged jury trials in Tasmania but my new diagnosis of terminal cancer has forced a more practical response from the prosecution. All charges dismissed: I am deemed gravely ill and neither innocent nor guilty, rather in legal limbo until my imminent death. Still, someone may want to read this sad tale and decide for themselves about my degree of naivety or complicity in what I see as a miscarriage of justice.

My parents were a sweet old couple, eighty-nine and ninety years old, well liked, with a large family, still fiercely independent despite burnt pots, falls and increasing frailty in recent years. They lived in Sandy Bay, one of Hobart's elite suburbs, and they grudgingly accepted some community-based support to help maintain the garden and keep their house clean. Their younger son, my brother Leigh, lived nearby and shouldered the load of appointments and shopping without complaint.

I was living in Phegans Bay on the New South Wales Central Coast during my parents' final years, working as a GP in nearby Woy Woy. My practice had evolved into caring principally for nursing home patients. As an ex-nurse, I got on well with the staff of residential aged care facilities and understood the problems of institutional care. Making myself available 24/7 by phone avoided many unnecessary emergency hospital presentations. Weekly rounds in each facility, with on-call visits as needed, avoided or solved many problems as they occurred.

It was a formula of care which worked well with family members, staff and residents and kept me very busy. Bulk-billing avoided any suggestion of over servicing. Living close to all the facilities made the workload possible. Referrals came from the local palliative care service and staff of the nursing homes to care for family members who were determined to die in their own homes, something I applauded and was happy to support with twenty-four-hour care. The doctors I worked with, knowing my predilection for providing home care, also referred many of their elderly housebound patients to me.

Only around ten per cent of my patients were seen in the clinic where I was based. It suited me to be out and about. I had never wanted to be stuck behind a desk. With a boot-load of equipment, I liked to solve problems as I drove from home to home; and, despite dealing with chronic illness and death, spreading optimism and cheer (or so I hoped) on my way.

I managed to get back to Hobart and family three or four times a year – birthdays and Christmas mainly – until my parents' final years, when my visits became more frequent, prompted by their falls and fractures and increasing decrepitude. On the final Christmas, Mother at eighty-nine was pushing herself around valiantly in a walker while Father at ninety was still getting about without a stick or frame, but with a clearly slowed and faltering gait that was hard to watch without jumping up to offer an elbow.

It's called 'furniture walking': grabbing bookshelves and sideboards in passing for surreptitious support. Again, all suggestions of assisted living options were dismissed by snorts. Serviced units, retirement villages? Never! Both pledged together to leave home in nothing but a wooden box.

In February 2016, my brother Leigh rang to tell me the police had informed him of the death of our brother Glendon, who worked as a teacher in Thailand. His body had been found on his bed a week after his demise. After hearing of the discovery, both my parents ceased eating and drinking, voluntarily fasting to end their lives.

I was unaware of their reaction until a week later when Leigh rang again to say he could see my father's teeth through his cheeks and that he couldn't get out of bed unaided or talk sensibly. It sounded like pre-morbid dehydration. My father was dying. I cancelled my work for a week and made a flight booking to Hobart the next morning.

Then I rang the local GP who had seen my father in the past week. I let him know of the recent developments with my father and my own area of work and familiarity with the dying. I expressed my desire to be with him and ease his passing and requested a few medications to help if needed when I arrived. I needed morphine to relieve any pain or shortness of breath and midazolam for agitation, distress and nausea. As it was a different state and I was not the treating doctor, the general practitioner involved was happy to help in the standard way.

Delirious and a little agitated, my father recognised me and, after some oral medication, settled quickly into a deep sleep. He had periods of abnormal breathing as had already been described to me by my brother. At first quite rapid and shallow, breaths would slow before ceasing altogether for a gap of ten to thirty seconds, then start again with a sudden gasp. And so the cycle would repeat itself. For those unfamiliar with death, this is called Cheyne-Stokes breathing and is typical of the final stage of life.

My father woke the next day still not talking clearly or coherently but fairly calm, sipping a little water, dozing on and off before returning to a deep sleep, when his breathing would again settle into the dying rhythm. Some writhing and calling out prompted a few doses of medication through the early morning but by half-past ten his long life was spent and he breathed his last in peace, in his own bed, his wife and two children with him.

CHAPTER TWO:
THE DEATH OF NELDA EDWARDS

OTHER THAN her grief and continued refusal to eat or drink, there was no sign that his wife, my mother, would join him only two days later. My father's death was neither unusual nor unexpected. His face in death was at peace but bore the signs of severe dehydration. The home visit from the local doctor was brief and my mother, well-dressed with just a touch of make-up, was restrained and declined any additional help or medication.

My father's body was soon removed to lie in a vat at the local university, awaiting dissection by medical students. At his age, one would think, his body would hold little interest for the organ bank. The rest of that day and the next passed in a sort of shock. Three sons, two wives and a few grandchildren wandered about the house murmuring appropriate replies as friends and neighbours called. Drinks were poured and Mother made sure nibbles were served while seeming slightly remote, aloof almost, politely declining offers of food for herself while toying with a brandy and dry. Passing me in a corridor, she whispered, 'I wish they'd all go away.'

We all tried, but Mother was determined not to eat or drink, and her habitual stubbornness had softened only slightly as her dementia advanced. 'Why don't you all go out to lunch?' she suggested the next afternoon during a lull between visitors. She would get herself something to eat and have a lie-down.

There she sat, smiling at us reassuringly, holding another half-glass of brandy and dry which someone had pushed on her with the last wave of cheese, crackers and beer. I think we all left for lunch believing she would eat, and we were all a bit tired of being confined together with too much of the cheese and nuts. When we returned, it looked unlikely Mother had eaten anything, despite her dismissive protest otherwise.

Then started the rosy 'future possibilities' talks. We sat with Mother together and separately, touting her greater financial stability, trying to find some shopping-and-cruise-inspired solace while offering the promise of greater involvement with grandchildren, of living with each of the children in turn, of supervised living options – but no. Mother's mind was made up. She would continue her fast until she joined Father.

'But Mum! You're doing so well. You've improved so much since your last fall.

You're walking much better …' Lies no-one believed. For someone who was once a champion Scrabble player, her new skill at word-finding puzzles was this time not praised. The day after her husband's death she would not be cheered. Visitors came and went. Mother accepted the condolences with grace while organising willing family members around her to serve and refresh drinks. Ice cubes clinked with abandon and sparkled in the sunlight flowing irreverently through the windows, regardless of the grief inside. Should the curtains be drawn? Looking around her living room of fine furniture and fresh flowers framing views of the river, Mother thought not.

I don't know how we got through that day. I had to withdraw to the guest bedroom with a beer a few times. Some of the visitors I hardly knew, it was all a bit much, but Mother remained courteous, smiling vaguely and crying a little with the hand-patting. It all seemed like some awful dream with no end.

When the last guest left, Mother announced she was going to bed. That was when my older brother, Robert, found the good Scotch. I don't remember if my mother's bedroom light was on or off when I stumbled past to my room a few hours later.

The next day was the day in question, the details of which would set off the malign suspicions of the deputy public prosecutor that would soon change my status as a doctor to that of a threat to the public, the day my mother died.

EVIL CONJECTURES

The events of that day as they unfolded would surround me with a whiff of conspiracy and complicity that led to my extradition from New South Wales two months later. Charged with matricide, I was to take a three-month sojourn in Risdon Prison, before finding myself on bail – a rare situation for someone accused of murder. I am only the second in Australia's history; a highly dubious distinction. The ongoing inquiry stretched out for a further four years, as investigations of both my parents' deaths and a possible family conspiracy crawled on. But that came later.

One the day my mother died, my parents' bedroom door was ajar when I woke, so I knocked and went in. My mother was sitting up in a bedjacket looking tired, a cup of cold tea untouched at her side. I sat on the end of the bed in one of my father's dressing gowns and asked her how she had slept. My mother was a chronic insomniac and would often get up in the night when we were children and scrub and wash the kitchen floor while baking a cake. Now she had medication packaged according to the time of day, including a sedative, but there had been arguments about continuing with them all since the fasting began. She swore she hadn't slept a wink all night, but then my brother Robert joined us and said he had crept into bed with her in the early hours for a cuddle.

'Oh yes,' she said, 'I thought it was your father.'

Would she like some more tea? No.

What would she like for breakfast? Nothing.

Then she started.

'Please, Stephen, give me something to help me sleep. I just want to rest properly.'

'Mum, you know I can't do that.'

'Yes, you can. You gave something to your father that let him sleep. Please, Stephen. Just a few hours.'

On and on she pleaded. She would feel better after a good sleep. No, she didn't want to see the doctor, another stranger in the house. You have the medicine here. Please, my mother begged.

Eventually I gave her a dose. Over the years I had promised to be there for both my parents at the end of their lives to help ease their passing if needed, but never to hasten death. Although their long-term support for assisted dying and Dr Philip Nitschke's magic pills was well known, the time for voluntary euthanasia was long past. Indeed, when the subject of their deaths came up, as it often did in their later years, and I offered my support, my father would admonish me not to do anything silly and get into any trouble. And I would heartily agree. Someone would joke about the car in the garage beneath the house, by then safely sold.

But this was just one dose. Five milligrams of the midazolam. A standard dose. My brothers came in and out, chatting with their coffees, Mother holding court, sitting up bright as a button. People continued to call and were politely steered away at the door. Daughters-in-law brought in vases of flowers until they filled the bedroom. Half an hour later mother complained of not the slightest drowsiness despite feeling a great weariness. Could she have some more, please?

I stalled, taking out cold tea and bringing back some iced water, but still she wanted more medication. Someone's suggestion of a stiff drink was declined crossly. The curtains were drawn and family withdrew while I sat, still in the dressing gown I had given my dad for a recent birthday, waiting for my mother to drop off. She didn't.

Another hour went by and, although a little slowed, my mother was resisting sleep and demanding another dose. It occurred to me that an old fractured lumbar vertebra might be troubling her. When I asked, she smiled up at me bravely and said it ached like hell. She never was one for painkillers but, with what I swore was the last dose of sedative, I gave her a little morphine syrup as well. I think it also helped to ease her resistance and relax. Soon she was sleeping soundly, moving her limbs a little now and then in the bed with contented murmurs.

And so the day passed. Family members congregated in a large kitchen/sitting room (distant from the bedroom) to where hushed visitors were ushered and food was dispensed with hot and cold drinks. Through it all, Mother slept on. I sat with her mostly, with others creeping in and out at intervals. In the afternoon I went out for an hour, for newspapers and comfort food, but on my return my mother's sleep was undisturbed.

It was not until late in the afternoon that her condition changed. It's hard for a practised doctor to hold a hand without feeling for the pulse.

Her's had been high all day: I had automatically attributed that to her chronic anaemia. This was caused by a longstanding condition common to the elderly called myelodysplasia, where the blood-producing bone marrow is slowly replaced by non-functioning fibrous tissue. Skipping any of her three medications to control her chronic high blood pressure would only have made her heart beat faster. Nelda was crafty enough to pop a few pills out of a blister pack and flush them down the sink. Who was to know?

It was around four o'clock when her heart rate began to slow and falter. Her movements in bed had also ceased. After half an hour it was clear something had happened; perhaps a heart attack, possibly a stroke. Certainly, she was dehydrated but not as severely as her husband had been and probably not enough to induce kidney failure, which is fatal but heralded by itching and slowly increasing drowsiness. Whatever had happened was serious. Her breathing became slower, then irregular, then fell into the awfully familiar rhythm of Cheyne-Stoking.

'What's happening?' asked the brothers. When I explained that our mother was entering the dying process my younger brother became very distressed. He had watched his mother-in-law for two days with the same pattern of stop–start breathing before she passed away in a nursing home only a year or two earlier. He retreated to the kitchen, vowing not to return.

Of course, there was talk of hospital but we all agreed that Mother would have hated the indignity, now that death was inevitable. We knew that, as an intensely private person, she would have loathed being carted off to hospital in an ambulance when she and our father had been adamant about dying in their own bed in their own home. They'd signed 'future directive' documents long ago declining life-prolonging procedures, but my mother's condition was now beyond any intervention other than comfort care.

When her groans started, I gave a little of the morphine and midazolam by injection that I had used with my father when he was unconscious but agitated. My reaction as a doctor was automatic and compassionate. My mother's grimacing and distress returned only once and I gave one further dose of the medications: standard medications used in nursing homes all around Australia at standard doses. My mother died peacefully an hour later.

It was nine o'clock on a Friday night. Three deaths in a week; we were all in shock. The on-call doctor would not visit to sign a death certificate, as it was an unexpected death. If Mother had seen the GP in the week since she had vowed not to eat or drink, considering her age and co-morbidities (the other chronic diseases she had accumulated), then the death would not have been unexpected; but our mother hated seeing doctors and, other than sitting in a waiting room, had not seen one for months. Because of this, the death became a coroner's case and we were told to call the police to have the body removed.

We explained that she had not eaten or drunk in a week since her son passed away unexpectedly in Thailand, that her husband had died because of not eating or drinking two days earlier and that I suspected dehydration and subsequent renal failure to have caused her death; not mentioning the use of medication as I spelled 'Cheyne-stoking' for their note-taking. I would rather explain my reasoning for using drugs to a doctor or a coroner than to the police. I felt sure I would be able to justify my actions face to face to anyone with medical knowledge of the dying process. This was the humane way doctors treated the dying: do nothing to hasten the process but relieve suffering when able.

On Monday the coroner's office suggested the case would not be heard for months, so I flew back to New South Wales to the solace of my partner and animals, home and garden. When my younger brother, Leigh, rang to report a police search of our parents' house I thought: Well, I had discarded the leftover morphine appropriately, emptying ampoules and syrup down a sink and putting the broken glass into recycling. My brother said the police went through the rubbish. What could be wrong with that?

Still, I was afraid. Too frightened to ring my medical insurer and report the case, I kept the worry to myself and tried to deal with the combined grief while throwing myself back into my work.

One hundred and fifty nursing home patients had not put their lives on hold and I had no formal arrangement with the other doctors I worked with to share the responsibility. When issues occurred while I was absent, the first doctor to take a nursing home call was obliged to deal with the problem. Of course, if a nursing home visit was not possible, the easy answer, the answer I avoided so many times, was call an ambulance and send them to hospital. Let them sort it out. But that's another story.

I was busy, which helped my busy mind. My partner and I flew back to Hobart the weekend after my parents' deaths for a subdued family gathering of all the grandchildren who were arriving from interstate to pay tribute to our parents and help sort the house contents. Neither of my parents was keen on funerals and both had bequeathed their bodies to science. I'm not sure our little wake did much to dispel the aching questions after three family members had died in a week. I remember feeling strangely guilty watching the young adults plundering our mother's jewellery, but returned nevertheless with a pair of my father's gold cufflinks, engraved with his initials, in my pocket.

Through the next few months the grief persisted, not helped by gnawing anxiety about the impending coroner's case. I worked long hours. I wrote and rewrote a long letter to a hypothetical coroner explaining my actions. I was also working hard at this time to master some ensemble pieces for an upcoming harp festival in France.

I was an active member of the Tasmanian Harp Society and we had been invited to play in a town in France where a factory produced many of the world's harps. Why the harp? Years earlier, I had returned to work in Tasmania after graduating from Sydney University and completing a further three years training as a GP in Sydney and rural New South Wales. I fancied myself as a country doctor and wanted to be nearby for my parents' sunset years. While living near a country town south of Hobart, I decided to take up the harp again. It was something I had tried for a year as a twenty-four-year-old while studying in London, and then abandoned. Serendipitously, an innovative harp-maker of world renown happened to live nearby. I found a teacher who was encouraging and introduced me to the Tasmanian Harp Society, a very welcoming fellowship. We enjoyed our workshops and concerts enormously.

It was this intended concert that led to my arrest and extradition to prison; but first, some more background.

CHAPTER THREE: THE ARREST OF STEPHEN EDWARDS

Sadly, the idea of living as a rural GP faded after working six months in New Norfolk and another three years in Huonville. The resilience of country folk was inspiring. 'Yeah, Doc, this leg is buggered but the other one is real good.' Still, something was missing. I couldn't settle.

My partner and I retreated to Hobart for a further year but even then I got cold feet while contemplating a mortgage on the south side of a hill in South Hobart. The winters were getting to me. I missed Sydney's weather and all the friends I had left behind. My parents seemed relatively stable …

We opted for Woy Woy, an hour by car or train from Sydney, and found a great house shaded by immense angophoras with a large overgrown garden hiding old stone paths on the top of a ridge in the midst of national parkland and overlooking the waterways below. It was heaven. That was before losing it to the lawyers.

After leaving the state, maintaining contact with the Tasmanian Harp Society was a pleasure. Flying backwards and forwards for rehearsals, concerts and masterclasses gave me an excuse to stay with my parents and monitor their slow decline. My father was diagnosed with advanced prostate cancer. My mother had a series of falls and fractures; one, leading to a bleed into the skull, needed burr holes to release increasing pressure on her brain from intracranial bleeding. On a background of dementia, her subsequent determination and eventual recovery of speech and walking were remarkable, but the days of cross-stitch and Scrabble were over. Her once finely rendered copperplate became a scrawl.

Keeping her safe and out of the kitchen were the priorities. Pottering in the garden led to a fractured hip a year later. Moving a too heavy flowerpot gave her a crush fracture in her lower spine. Despite all our beseeching for caution and moderation, her cavalier attitude was only accentuated by the dementia. As children she had admonished us all repeatedly to put her out of her misery if she ever became batty. She had seen others in their dotage and insisted she be hit in the back of the head with a brick if the same fate befell her.

Fortunately, dementia is mostly kind, and our mother had no insight into her developing childlike state or much regret for lost skills. She was once an excellent gardener and cook. Her gardens always won praise. My younger brother struggled to control the garden so that the weeding and pruning were not so pressing, but sweeping leaves was an imperative hard to ignore.

When the date of the harp festival in France was only a few weeks away and I had still not heard anything about a forthcoming hearing, I rang the coroner's office. They were conciliatory and suggested another six months' wait at least. They also suggested I inform the Tasmanian Police. The police were similarly reassuring about leaving the country, suggesting a wait of between six and twelve months before resolution of the case and supporting my proposed departure for a week or two.

On 29 April 2016, only two days later, my life changed forever. At eight in the morning there was a loud knock on the door. Two Tasmanian police officers stood there with an additional two from the local station. Can we have a word?

All smiles, a man and woman, they were both charming. Just a few questions to set the story straight and lay it to rest at the nearby police station where it can be recorded. Just to settle the matter. Shouldn't take long. It seemed so reasonable, them standing there in the living room admiring the view. One of our cats was not so easily taken in, however, and promptly urinated at their feet.

The interview lasted five hours. My explanations were accepted. The presence of pro-euthanasia material discovered in my parents' house search (a newspaper article by an advocate with Dr Nitschke's name underlined) led to suggestions ranging from hoarded sedatives by my mother, to assisted suicide. I scoffed at these ideas and felt, in the end, that I had convinced them both that my mother, on a background of chronic disease with poorly controlled blood pressure complicated by dehydration after a week of refusing food or fluid, had succumbed to either a heart attack or a stroke and died as a result. They seemed happy to let me go. I had a busy afternoon in the clinic and felt a little relieved that evening. Was I now free to grieve?

The next morning, while talking to staff in a nursing home, a receptionist arrived breathlessly to inform me that three police officers were outside and were wishing to have a word, and to bring my bag. Nothing was said about arrest. We need you to come back to the station. I don't remember if a hand pushed my head down like in the movies as I was placed into the back seat of one of the waiting cars.

The drive to Sydney was smooth but not very chatty. It was after consulting with the deputy public prosecutor the previous evening that my guilt had been decided. I wasn't handcuffed until delivered to the central Sydney holding facility in Darlinghurst. There I was offered a single cell or a group cell. 'For company,' the desk sergeant suggested. Listening to the screams of the ice addicts raging as they came down overnight made me thankful for my solitude in my choice of a single cell.

I was grateful to be allowed to call my partner from the airport the next day. Tasmania-bound, I needed to tell him where I'd left our car. 'It's all a misunderstanding. I'll be back soon.' At sixty-one years of age, after a blameless life of helping others, I was on my way to prison.

After some registration processing at the holding facility in Hobart, I was cuffed again and pushed into a claustrophobic police bus. Six metal boxes with a small metal grill in each door, and just enough room to sit on a metal bench but not enough room to stand, only crouch. No paper tissues or complimentary packets of nuts, I later learned that prisoners on remand travelled from Hobart to Launceston and Burnie, anything from two to four hours, for court appearances in these cramped metal boxes in bone-shaking buses with suspension not designed for the reinforced metal and human cargo above.

We swept across the bridge and bounced up the river through increasingly gloomy suburbs until reaching Risdon Prison itself. Stripped and outfitted in shapeless green, I was deemed a suicide risk and escorted to the high risk/special observation wing. Little did I know that soon I would be losing at checkers to mass murderer Martin Bryant.

CHAPTER FOUR: JAIL TIME

WHAT WAS IT like in prison? 'Did I get bashed or abused?' people ask, in hushed voices. Not knowing if or when my release was coming was the hardest thing. Would it ever end? My legal team were suitably optimistic.

All the big and little ways that prisons work to dehumanise the inmates belongs to a Dickensian world long overdue for radical reform. What percentage of the jail population was like me, awaiting judgement? On remand, if you don't get bail, you're presumed guilty. The court backlog means that cases may not be heard for two years or more. By the time the prisoner goes to court the term of incarceration in the sentence may have already been served. The official response? Tough.

I spent my first six weeks in the Mersey unit, a high suicide-risk, high-observation block, seventeen cells with a rolling population of the mentally unstable. It took three weeks for me to lose my pompous indignance. An old hand took me aside in the common area and paced with me in the exercise yard. Don't rattle the bars, he would say. Play along. How are you today? Living the dream!

Although his neighbours hadn't been fond of him mowing his suburban lawn in the middle of the night, he had somehow survived ice and was neither unhinged nor drug-fucked. Always with too much energy, he told me that when he was at school his teachers would give up and send him outside to help the gardener. He learned to read and write on his first stint inside playing Scrabble.

This time he was in prison accused of the murder of another ice dealer. The criminal he took out was much hated by the police, who were keen to protect my new friend from other inmates affiliated with his victim until the case went to court. The funny-bin was, for him, a safe refuge. He slept well.

The groans, screams and other anguished cries of the criminally insane locked in their small cages would echo around the bare walls of the barrack most nights. We would wake to animal howls, then the bashing and crashing noises, then more screams as the guards arrive, sounds of a quick scuffle, then a muffled exit to one of the three padded cells in the compound provided for their comfort. There were some guards who, it was clear, enjoyed these nightly rituals. When called to strong-arm a distressed resident by day, their laughter and bonhomie were disgusting. We all looked down.

Those who had not slept so well were given distance when the cell doors opened in the morning and we moved into the common area. Milling around the toaster and microwave when breakfasts arrived, wry comments would be made about whoever had gone off in the night. It was often ice addicts who needed a week after arriving in prison to withdraw from the drug and find whatever level of brain function remained. Fourteen days, my friend advised. After not sleeping for over fourteen days your brains are permanently fried.

The revolving door of Risdon Prison does nothing to prevent this cycle of self-destruction. Perhaps a prison farm would be more helpful than incarceration? Then there are all the victimless crimes. Marijuana cultivators, known as *croppers*, are a good example. How much does it cost to lock them up to do hospital laundry? I heard between four and five hundred dollars a day. Perhaps a prison farm would be more appropriate?

During my stay in the loony-bin I had regular meetings with the mental health team when I would rage against the system, the lack of access to the prison library, a two-week delay before my partner Jamie could be approved for phone calls, having a torch shone in my eyes every hour overnight through the cell door to ensure I hadn't topped myself. I ranted at them in high dudgeon, outraged, innocent, frustrated and furious.

The phone access came, the library did start sending me books and, with my murderer friend's counselling, I chose a lower profile: not docile but reticent. Hearing the personal stories of my (erstwhile) companions made me feel less self-important. Although I protested my innocence, my fellow inmates assumed my guilt which gave me unexpected kudos. *Murd* sits at the top of the criminal hierarchy. At the bottom are the paedophiles, who have to be housed separately in their own barracks for protection from the other inmates and known as *tamps* (those who tamper).

The first question to newcomers is, 'What are you in for?' My story spread quickly. Soon, people were addressing me as Doc or The Doc. I played along and would do crazy faces. It would get a laugh. I had been handed an easy persona to maintain which, as an older and much affected man, saved me from any other abuse when moved to the general prison. My friend would say in company, in a way I found charming and disarming, that I couldn't kill anyone without a script pad. When a young inmate informed me with a snigger that I was a sick cunt, it took me a moment to realise he was *complimenting* me.

13 May 2016: Random acts of injustice reduced us to insolent animals. A small toothbrush I cleaned my cell with went missing. During my cell inspection a few days later, I asked the guard whom I knew had removed my handle-less brush why it had been taken. He said, how do you know? I replied that it could not have been removed by a resident. Re-entering my cell after inspection by this particular guard a few mornings earlier, I could see he had walked into my wet shower area and then through the cell, spreading dirty footprints throughout the tiny space. My prison-issue toothbrush sat by the metal sink. The extra stub of a toothbrush saved from my night in Hobart Remand Centre and normally out of sight, but this day left out in the shower area, had gone.

He informed me that I had *attitude* and was *condescending*. Other guards had remarked on the spotlessness of my cell. OK, I am a bit obsessive with cleaning. Blame my mother, no dust on her venetians! I couldn't sit with a newspaper in a garden without jumping up to remove a few dead leaves, and then maybe clear some dead branches while I'm at it. When I had a lot on my mind, I found some brutal pruning to be wonderfully therapeutic.

Hence, in the lengthy periods locked in my cell I set upon all the lumpy yellowing stains, the excrement of many years of lonely souls around the bunk and up the once white walls. Who could blame me? The black scuff marks on the floor and door disappeared easily with my soapy toothbrush.

Request forms were needed for many little and big things. My trousers were too loose and I was always pulling them up. When I requested something better fitting, I received smaller pants, short in the leg and with a large hole. Keep smiling! Despite requests, a second pillow required a little sleight of hand. Luxury!

When a long-anticipated bail hearing arrived, it was not until I had waited an hour in the cells beneath the Supreme Court that I was informed that the hearing was delayed by the prosecution's ongoing investigation into the possible murder of my *father*. Patricide!

The judge required extra time to consider the evidence. The junior of my legal team gave me the news in a grim room with two chairs and a metal table under a caged light bulb. Soon I was back in the metal box in the prisoner transport bus, brimming with righteous indignation.

I think it's extraordinary, I wrote that night, referring to the deputy public prosecutor who was investigating my father's death as possible murder, that someone with no idea of the dying process could desecrate the memory of my father with such a vile and evil conjecture. It's outrageous. It is so far removed from the truth. It's an unqualified and foul idea from someone who should be reprimanded.

Well, that's not going to happen. When the case was dropped, it was made clear that if I made waves the Tasmanian Police would make my remaining life miserable. But more of that later …

It was time to write to the Ombudsman, the Governor, the Attorney-General and the press. I wrote. My legal team read the letters and advised against sending any. Be patient!

Bide my time. Ha! When does mad as hell become just mad? Focusing my anger at the person who decided to bring me back to Tasmania (Risdon Prison) while further investigating the case against me for matricide and then extending that to patricide was not a healthy option. Linda Mason, assistant public prosecutor, was said to be like a dog with a bone. Her job description is as follows: 'Responsible to the Director of Public

Prosecutions for the prosecution of complex, novel, sensitive and critical criminal matters on behalf of the State of Tasmania before the Court of Criminal Appeal, Supreme Court, Magistrates Court and Tribunals.' Her self-professed guiding principle was a quote by Dr Tom Barratt, 'The more clearly someone sees the future, the more confidently they work in the present.' She obviously saw an assisted suicide at least, and possibly a doctor who helped many others along to a quick exit.

All my books of death certificates for my New South Wales patients were taken as evidence, and in the indictment I was branded a threat to the public. Hatred was not the answer. I didn't want an ulcer and couldn't see the cancer coming.

1 June 2016: Another grim day and the first day of winter. Its dry but a cold wind is blowing. I am cheered by the number of cards from well-wishers I receive each morning, but when a severely brain-damaged inmate starts mumbling to himself in the lead-up to a dummy spit, I crack and ask to be returned to the peace of my cell until lunch.

I had already approached the guards for request forms. I wanted one for the 'therapeutic team' to move me to Roy Fagan, the minimal security unit where access to the library is allowed and cells can be entered and left as desired. Comfortable chairs are available for sitting and reading. Imagine! My friend was moving there soon and advised me to ask the team to facilitate my reclassification and transfer.

Access to a football oval in minimum security didn't thrill me and I was a bit creeped out, as they say, by a tale about a local dog charity which provided rescue dogs to the lonely inmates of Roy Fagan until the project had to be abandoned after it was found the dogs were learning new skills and getting a bit too much love.

My eldest brother, who visited once a week, had been seeing a psychologist for the first time regarding his difficulty grieving for our parents and dealing with my imprisonment. During our last meeting he had told me I should see a psychologist myself. They were available in the prison, he'd checked. So sweet! I discovered much later that the therapeutic team were contacted by family members expressing concern over my mental health – how I hate that expression! – and stability. I guess we all do what we think best.

I put in a request for new socks. Somehow one of my two pairs got switched in the laundry to one with large hole in a larger threadbare area. Unfortunately, the guards are all out of request forms. The computer to generate more is offline and the photocopier is not working – all explained with smiles close to sneers.

Today is the day we get the weekly inmate news, a rubbishy collection of useless information with a TV guide from Monday to Sunday, leaving two days uncharted as the 'news' comes out on a Wednesday. Don't complain! That's how it's done here. You're in jail now.

The story from the inmates was that a new prison director had been appointed, a reformer from the UK who produced an agenda to lead the jail into a bright new future. The guards objected, the system groaned and each item of reform was stymied by the this-is-how-we-do-it-here attitude, the keep-your-smart ideas-to-yourself response. If it kind of works, leave it alone. It's a Tasmanian thing, our ball and chain.

The new director resigned in protest but is yet to be replaced, or so the story goes. Oddly, he shares my surname and lives half a block from my younger brother, who once returned his Alsatian puppy; but that's Tasmania, as they say. I wonder what he thought when my request for a harp in my cell crossed his desk. It went to an underling before, a month later, I received a reply.

'Re request for harp … your request has not been approved on this occasion.'

That same afternoon I met up with my soon-to-be-leaving friend who made me feel like a slow learner. Every time I spit the dummy and ask to be put back in my cell during out-of-cell time it's held as a mark against me, he explained.

A woman who knew me too well had written in a card, 'No hissy fits!' And that's just what had happened that morning.

'That man is disgusting. No, he's a train wreck.'

'So what?' my friend said. 'If he picks his scalp scabs off all the time, talks to himself – loudly and incomprehensibly – drinks all our milk with his compulsive coffee and Milo consumption while drawing guns or cars? If he rants, avoid him. It's not the guard's fault he is in the wrong place.'

When I came out for lunch a female guard commented, 'You look better now.'

And I replied, 'Yeah. They just get to me sometimes. There's so many in here now with different degrees of brain damage.'

'I've seen it much worse than this,' she countered.

My friend added later that the guards write reports on all of us every day, including any inmate requesting in-cell time.

At unlock time a few mornings ago one of the guards said to me, 'How are you today?' To which I replied, 'Well, I've got no newspaper, no books and I'm surrounded by brain damage.' To which another guard laughed, 'Yeah, you're in jail now.'

'That's about it,' I snapped back, trying not to spin on my heel or storm off.

'Not the right attitude,' my friend says. 'Smile and wave. Be helpful. Be pleasant. Be *nice*.'

When I said to the guard that two of the people here who could hold a conversation were leaving for different areas soon, she said, 'If you can stay like this, you'll be able to leave as well.'

Well, that's damn obvious now you say it.

A photo of my parents in full cocktail-party mode had been published in the local paper the day after my arrest and had been saved by my murderous friend for my arrival. Using this, stuck to some cardboard and lit only by the green glow from the TV screen set to a disconnected channel, I tried to silently invoke the help of my newly dead ancestors in getting me out of this fine mess. Careful to sit cross-legged before my eerie altar only after the hourly guard check, only once did I seem to see the flicker of my mother's nightgown as she passed, after which I gave up on seances.

I did, however, dream a lot. In one dream I saw my father standing in a room full of men chatting informally. When I reached his side, he turned to me and I said, 'Dad, can you get me out of here?'

He looked around the room vaguely and then said, 'Yes, I think I can.' That was all I could remember in the morning but I clung to that dream. I never lost hope but the daily bullying inherent in the system did get me down.

Tick-tock, ignore the clock! Was I going spare? I wondered in my spotless cell as I tried not to chase the fluff as it floated across the polished concrete floor but waited for it to gather in corners.

15 June 2016: Six-and-a-half weeks in. I wrote, 'I hate the boredom, the food, the television, a lot of the company, and the tendency to overeat as compensation for all of the above. I particularly hate the legal system …' And on I went. 'I read, I write, I pace the exercise yard, I attend a gym, totally out of character, feeling sane but on the verge of a nervous breakdown, at risk of losing hope and lapsing into despair, looking down at the dark pit of despond yawning at my feet …'

I watch the moon come up through my barred window. Somehow it reassured me. With a chair leaning back in the shower bay I could read in real sunlight for a few hours a day and watch the clouds. I wanted to draw the weeds outside my window which often struck me as profoundly beautiful; not the sort of thought to share in the common room.

22 May 2016: Today I craved beer and cigarettes, so I had an extra bowl of bran with soy milk as a low-calorie, bulking agent to fill the void, and drank more water than usual. The screws have been especially irritating …

One of the loopier residents decided to take his pants off while walking in the exercise yard. It was an unusually calm and sunny day a week before winter. He had briefs and runners on, yet after an ice addict with the fried-brain syndrome lost it and threw the microwave oven across the common room a few days earlier, it wasn't the craziest behaviour. We were, after all, male. No-one was especially bothered or confronted. He was a bit odd, anyway, so no-one made a fuss; but after a few minutes, two other inmates came out into the yard to tell us that the screws disapproved and wanted him to put his track pants back on.

He couldn't see why. Nor could we. I was sitting at a table in the sun with an open book. Two other prisoners were also walking laps and a few other guys were just mooching around. We were all chatting, all very low key until two guards came out and demanded that the pants were put back on and that he would have to go back to his cell.

He put his pants on, thinking that was all that was necessary, but the guards said, no, you ignored our request. You now have to go back to your cell.

He didn't make a fuss. There was no point, but it seemed a bit over the top. The warning had been delivered second-hand. Now the guards were being obnoxious. Nobody complained.

Maybe twenty minutes later, the same guards came back out into the still sunny exercise area where the same five or six of us were walking or sitting around. One of the guards indicated the weighted exercise balls; two five-kilogram and two ten-kilogram rubber balls with handles that a fifty-year-old inmate had been using with gusto quite a lot, along with a few others keen to increase muscle mass. My efforts with the balls were much more subdued, but now they were sitting on the ground.

'No-one seems to be using these,' said one of the guards. 'They might as well be flowerpots,' he added to his colleague.

We all said nothing. Hardly cutting repartee, I thought. They shared some nasty laughter, then went back inside. Compared with the pushing and shoving we endured which they so enjoyed, this was minor stuff. We milled about and eventually fell into a supportive cluster at my table for some subdued growling about the screws, wondering if they had microphones outside to hear our disgruntled talk. I suggested their behaviour was influenced by undersized appendages. The others were more floridly disdainful. Someone referred to written instructions given to new residents which admonished us to treat others as we wished to be treated. So much for that. They had the power.

We had to be meek, which caused me much rancour. Amongst my murderous and otherwise criminal companions, I felt that my underlying innocence only served to increase my tendency to take offence at the embedded dehumanising tactics of guards. There was, in the end, only one solution. Get over it!

I bought up the issue of frayed wires in the handholds of the weighted machines in the gym. These wires could easily pierce the skin. The gym attendant said he'd look into it. The next week, gym outings being only a weekly treat, I again pointed out the projecting ends of bare wires in the handholds, politely adding that the incidence of hepatitis C in prison would be much higher than in the general population. How long would a spot of blood remain contagious? I mused. He'd look into it. Now, with my fellows, I threatened to make a complaint to higher authorities as some sort of bravura from the beaten, but someone pointed out it could well backfire and the authority that controlled us could easily suspend our gym use for a while.

Further passive-aggression? Hmmm. Not unlikely. The sun clouded over and people drifted inside to wait for dinner to arrive. I did a few more laps before going in, invoking my father's memory to walk with me awhile until I calmed down.

Yesterday afternoon a new guard to our crazy block asked a colleague how many of the inmates were on medication.

'All of them,' was the reply

'I'm not.' I interjected

'Not yet.'

I met a bloke called Bill who was in the close observation unit, Risdon Prison's funny-farm, when I arrived there myself. He was not there because he was suicidal, just too stupid to survive in the general prison population. I don't know if he was born brain-damaged, or if it was an acquired brain injury, but he was a forty-year-old puppy. Everyone gave him room. The guards would even help him clean his cell while other messy residents copped abuse. Bill was happiest playing his racing car games on an Xbox, loudly, at all hours.

Outside, Bill had lived alone in housing department units. Plural, because when Bill became upset or angry, he would burn his flat, be charged with arson, malicious damage, whatever, and be sent to jail. Once his time was served, he would be rehoused until he next got upset.

I don't know how many times he had been in and out of prison. When I knew him, he was getting escorted day leave once a week to 'reacclimatise' him to life outside. He would return in time for dinner, excited by some new purchase. Once it was more car games from the tip shop. He played them all that night. Sometimes, if people had been unkind, or he had been up late, the guards would have to coax him out of his cell in the mornings. Sometimes they wouldn't bother. When he did come out into the common area he would move from group to group, eager to share a joke or join a conversation.

Once, one of the men in a small cluster was sounding off about someone outside who had done him wrong and how he would get even when his time here was done. Bill, who was getting out soon anyway, jumped in to offer to go around to their house and burn it down for them.

The men sat back from their huddle, but no-one laughed. 'No, no, that's OK.' The man countered.

'No, no,' Bill answered, tail wagging, so eager to please. 'Just give me her address.'

I was getting the *Guardian Weekly* and the daily local paper. Delivery started well, but then became sporadic until it ceased altogether. Of course, I complained, complained and complained, filling out daily requests until the well-thumbed newspapers reappeared with the many cards each morning.

The local paper was always popular, often giving early warning of new arrivals with details from the court of the latest illegal high jinks, followed in a day or two by the antihero's arrival in our midst. Much back-clapping.

An elderly recidivist with few remaining teeth, but a private education, would quietly complete any unfinished crosswords in the papers I left out for others to pore over. Embarrassed to be back inside, he was soon moved to the general area but not before thrashing me at Scrabble.

Checkers and chess were popular and, yes, I did play checkers with Martin Bryant, where again I was trounced despite the high levels of medication he was on. A docile animal who often had to be coaxed from his cell in the mornings, he had a history of repeated self-harm. Time spent in the prison hospital resulted in a stultifying drug cocktail which removed his ability to commit suicide and rendered him almost mute.

Still, new inmates would get him excited with questions about where to buy guns and which ones he liked. He was not tall. The drugs and prison diet had increased his weight. Recent recognition in the visitors' centre with his mother on his birthday led to abuse and food-throwing from other inmates. Since then, he has shaved his long, curling, blond locks and now looks like a stumbling Tweedledee who could still wipe the floor with me at checkers.

Prison haircuts were a common-room activity of some entertainment value. Electric clippers were available from the guard's desk and people would shave their scalps to stubble before court appearances or after a few weeks of settling in. Sometimes an old hand would play the barber. It was a form of ritual cleansing, or leaving the outside world behind. Almost an initiation into prison life, all signs of previous charisma were shaved away. You're in jail now. No hair gel here. I let my curls grow long and lank, saying I'd wait until I got out.

Diary entry 13 June 2016: I am becoming numb to the horror. Eating bread, margarine and honey in the kitchen at 4am as someone half-yells, half-screams somewhere. It's like a prison call to prayer. Wake up! You're in jail, and not mad. Yet. How many others are lying in the dark listening to the incoherent anguish? I watch video hits. I write about all the schizophrenics I've known. The screaming stops and I consider a bit of a nap before lights go on for muster, but there he goes again.

I learned to keep my head down. People would approach me for advice about minor and major ailments and I was happy to share my knowledge. It put me in good stead, although I often felt like a nurse offering a calm ear in a psychiatric ward. I found myself interpreting medical reports embedded in crumpled legal documents and filling out medical request forms, amusing myself by using medical terminology and succinctness way beyond the inmate's comprehension.

When the mental health team finally decided that I had settled in and was now deemed a low suicide risk, I was moved to the general cell blocks. Medium security meant no torch in the face at night. The next step would be transfer to minimal security, where inmates tended to be older and laptops were permitted.

Not that I wanted that. Entertaining dreams of a transfer seemed like the route to failure, of acquiescence, of giving up any idea of redemption and settling for silence, subservience and, if I'm really good, a harp in my cell. Oh no, I wanted my innocence declared, my freedom restored and a public apology from someone. Not necessarily the Queen; any grovelling dignitary would do.

When I arrived in medium security, I found my story had spread. People I didn't know would say 'Hey, Doc!' with a deferential nod in passing. Huge muscle-builders would ask me for advice about tendon injuries and whatnot. I didn't mind, and would get a laugh with my frank manner. A few good diagnoses and successful home remedies raised my profile amongst the thugs. Other than that, I minded my own business and kept to myself. I wrote. I meditated – something I had learned on retreats in my twenties – which kept me sane in the funny-farm when the head-banging started in the dead of night.

18 June 2016: I keep my face closed, my voice low and expressionless. I do not exist. I am no-one. Twelve days till hearing …

There were five barracks in the main yard, each with four cell blocks, two up and two down, seven cells in each with one a double – two bunks, twice the size – and generally with only one occupant, sometimes myself, in deference to my age and former status, I liked to think.

The downside was finding myself suddenly sharing the space with a newbie. Once it was with a young lad coming down from an extended ice binge. Poor man couldn't sleep without the TV on. I'd turn it off when he went to sleep; he'd turn it back on when I went to sleep. His colourful history of home invasions was something I overheard from a phone conversation with his legal aid, not from cheerful chats over tea and biscuits. Thankfully, he was moved to a barracks where more of his friends were resident.

As inmates entered and left the cell blocks, heavy outer doors would slam shut with a loud boom. The slamming of these doors, four per block, would go on and on until lockdown, reverberating around all the cells. One resident with a sore head swore at me, 'Can't you stop slamming the fucking door?' But unless their closing was closely controlled, that's what they did. Slam with two or three smaller reverberations afterwards as it bounced closed. All day. Every day. First a loud click as the door is pushed open, then a loud boom with one or two echoes as it slams shut. Every time. Alone inside your own cell, you'd wait for it. Focus on it. All four doors in the block were audible, one louder than the rest. Relentless. Don't complain! You're in prison, you know. Think of something else to stop the echoing in your skull jangling through every nerve, on and on, over and over: Boom, boom, boom. Boom, boom, boom. Boom, boom, boom.

Each unit has seven cells, one a double-up. Usually, one or two were empty and kept locked. Often, they would be locked while residents were elsewhere, off to a court hearing at the top of the state or having a stint in the Mersey, the suicide-watch unit, after expressing black thoughts to the 'therapeutic team'. Perhaps some misdemeanour occasioned a break in solitary.

Small TVs were supplied to each inmate but were in short supply. After endless requests lodged with the unit sergeant produced nothing, the men in my unit, in the spirit of goodwill and whatever else they were using, decided to help out and nick one from an unused but unemptied cell, thereby demonstrating the fine art of cell door break-ins.

I witnessed a number of these in Rowallan, my first unit after the funny-farm. Hearing a subdued ruckus one evening, I emerged from my cell to investigate on the way to the kitchen. Well, it was hard to ignore. The finesse of the two-man effort was ingeniously entertaining. A broom handle was used to force the door from the frame at the inner upper end. With a gap created, string was introduced bit by bit until the end was retrieved from beneath the door. A plastic thong was then attached and fed back into the cell. By manipulating the two ends of string at great speed to make it look easy, the thong would eventually catch and depress the inner door handle which, with a foot kept pressed against the bottom of the door, would allow it to spring open.

It was a remarkable feat accomplished silently and at great speed. Like birds piercing metal milk bottle caps, the process was learnt and shared. In my last unit I watched a new team orchestrated by an old hand. The lack of finesse was embarrassing, with much cursing, lost broom handles and jammed fingers. Multiple attempts failed until the intercom crackled and the guards suggested we desist.

How was life in gaol? Here is another diary entry.

4 May 2016: There is one bloke here I met early on in the psych bin. He's a gentle soul; someone you'd trust with your sick baby while popping out to the pub. He'd been in high observation for a few months before I arrived, mostly because of a strongly held intention to top himself if things went against him. He is quite philosophical about it and otherwise comes across as a lovely chap, quite funny at times.

He is in for attempted murder. After a few weeks he showed me the hospital report. Multiple stab wounds, all fairly superficial, all to one side of the body only. She had been driving at 110km/h from one end of the island to the other. During that time, he sat next to her and had repeatedly stabbed her.

'Just a pocket knife,' he said. He'd been suspicious for a few months and had finally confirmed her infidelity via some quick chat site – something with no stored memory, but a few photos had been saved, giving the game away.

Dave is in his early fifties and works out with weights every day to keep himself trim. I used to give him my serves of Milo so he'd get my washing done before lunch, allowing me an extra shower during lunchtime lockdown.

A bikie with terrible teeth, he'd had the top row removed and was waiting for the swelling to subside before having an impression taken for the dentures. He was quite excited by the prospect. Apparently, the jail would provide them for only a few hundred dollars, compared with thousands on the outside.

I was often doing speed-walking laps of the exercise yard, keeping my eyes on the distant hills and humming to myself. *Summertime*; 'Swing Low, Sweet Chariot, comin' for to carry me home'; old Hare Krishna chants – whatever came to mind. So what, if they think I'm losing it? Dave would join me sometimes for a desultory chat. He would tell me which country towns were heavily into ice, other inmate gossip, which female guards he fancied.

One day he was very excited but also quite worried. His charge had been reduced to wounding, presumably malicious, although there is probably no category for casual or non-serious wounding. His problem was the backlog in sentencing.

The problem for Dave was that when he was finally sentenced, he might qualify for early release, and this could occur before his dentures were ready. With poor enunciation, he insisted he would prefer to stay the extra time until his new teeth arrived.

I met him later on in medium. We shared a unit for a while but his mood slipped and he disappeared back to the high-observation unit.

Prison life started at 7am with a brutally loud, highly distorted and mostly unintelligible recorded wakeup call via intercom. We had fifteen minutes to shower, clean our cells and be ready for muster. Then breakfast would arrive. At ten-to-eight, the cells were inspected before the outer door was opened. At eleven o'clock, we returned to our barracks for re-inspection and the lockdown of each cell block during lunch.

At twelve-thirty, we were re-inspected and let out for the afternoon. At three-thirty, general unit cleaning was expected and inspected at four o'clock with the last muster and evening lockdown.

When the unit was unlocked, inmates were free to wander around the grounds and move in and out of the other barracks and reacquaint themselves with old friends. Small groups would form into boot camps, with much huffing and puffing as they tried to reform their bodies in defiance of their pasts.

One muscle-bound, middle-aged specimen liked to pound a punching bag attached to the fire escape of my cell block. The whole building seemed to shake. He had the big, gnarly hands and solid body of an ex-boxer. A bit doughy around the waist from beer and age, but still firm with legs like tree-trunks and arms you could hang off. His punching bag routine had the fire escape shaking and clanging loudly through the entire block.

Never once did I ask him to fuck off with his hopeless quest for youth, beauty or the ability to bound over barbed-wire-topped fences in a single leap. I didn't even look at him, for fear of what he might say.

In the Mersey unit I was introduced to *planking*, a form of isometric endurance exercise performed by lying straight with only the head and ankles supported. Often demonstrated in the yard, it was a fun diversion I reserved for the long hours alone in my cell.

New boys on the block would often sport grazes and black eyes in the first weeks of settling in. Not interested in learning new skills, I kept mostly to myself, but there was a docile cropper in our block, a champion of victimless crime and an intriguing authority on natural and synthetic hallucinogens with whom I would sometimes chat. An old hand, he was heavily involved in a complex barter system involving food and other items available for purchase. Prisoners received a fortnightly stipend of a few dollars, augmented by symbolic 'wages' for laundry work to buy shavers and whatnot at inflated prices. He would also happily illuminate murky areas of prison etiquette for me. Always perfectly shaved beneath his long hippy locks, he was also rather unguardedly opinionated about the personal hygiene of others in our unit until he acquired a black eye and lost his opinions.

3 June 2016: Yesterday I received from the chaplain a sixty-page photocopied book on the Vipassanā meditation technique, the same teachings I received in my twenties. I've read half already and am thrilled to have it with me now. It is helpful to review my practice. Esoteric knowledge in my hands! The road to enlightenment here in my grasp! Again, I say to myself, aren't I fortunate?

26 June 2016: I have to stop reading Raymond Carver. His depressing tales are not helping my mood at all.

Today was my first day working in the prison laundry, not the worst place to be on a very chilly day. Someone found me an extra pullover and my cold hands were soon warmed by folding hospital towels fresh from the dryers. The old hands were quite cheerful, but the ogre of my bin was in a particularly foul mood on waking and I was soon the focus of his venom.

With no idea how to respond, the others tried to deflect his ire from me until, with a loud expression of disgust, he called me 'Big Bird' and turned away, which allowed everyone to laugh and the tension to dissolve. Being tall with a bit of a stomach developing and large feet that face more sideways than forward, I thought the Big Bird analogy was an inspired, if perhaps unintentional, means of defusing the situation.

The other inmates went on to outdo each other and draw catcalls with feats of strength and prowess as they larked about among the trolleys and huge machines, living the dream. A fat overseer sat behind a wall of glass and watched over the crew of crooks who cavorted about his theatre of work and play. My second day in the laundry, I stayed with sorting the trolleys filled with hot material from the dryers. As I got some steam up, I started flinging assorted items onto the folding tables over and between the heads of those folding. Fitted sheets, theatre coats and hospital gowns flew from my arms until the work flagged and I could wander about watching others at their various stations.

Three days before winter solstice the notorious Bridgewater Jerry, a low fog formation that drifts down the River Derwent around Hobart from a down-at-heel suburb up-river (after which it is named) didn't lift. The first anti-Tasmanian joke (of which there are many) that I heard on returning to the isle as a doctor was, what do Bridgewater girls use for protection? The answer was bus shelters.

The fog wouldn't dissipate but hovered gloomily over the river all day. In the midst of the day, someone told me of a doctor recently interred in Risdon for the mercy killing of his wife. Apparently, he topped himself, hence perhaps my prolonged sojourn in the crazy-bin. Six weeks surrounded by nutters because they are worried about me. How sweet!

Someone in the laundry mentioned astral travelling. Funny. I woke for some blessed meditation in the quiet hour before morning muster. Forget blame and recrimination, I thought. Hello, astral travelling, conscious dreaming, meditation, conjuring ancestors – it seemed like a whole new world of exploration that I have been preparing for in my past sixty-one years. Thank you, world!

God, I'd like a hot bath. Too much noise from the boys to entertain meditation now. I walk to and from the bathroom. Savage voices echo from a cell where a new boy sits with an old bully, blustering on together like a school reunion. News of friends and exploits on the outside; why should I disparage their mutual maintenance of spirits in this hellhole? Let them be!

Still, the constant bluster and bravado of the common room accompanied by all the exaggerated strutting, swaggering, profuse blasphemy and thigh-slapping bursts of callous laughter was exhausting, and best appreciated from the inside of a firmly closed cell door. Who am I to remind or disillusion them of their rather constrained circumstances? As a means to maintain a semblance of power in such a disempowered state, to cling to their sanity rather than fall into despair, such behaviour was understandable. These were men keen to show they could make their own fun and come out of captivity uncowed by the prison system, or in spite of it. I did, however, look forward with sweet anticipation to a time when *fuck* would not be the most frequently used expletive. Fuck that, as they say.

28 June 2016: I queue with a cup half-filled with water for my morning medication. While others receive antidepressants and antipsychotics, I have a vitamin D capsule dropped into my palm through a grate in a barred door.

After swallowing it, I turn to the guard by the door and open my mouth to demonstrate the medication is taken, not secreted.

'Lift your tongue!'

I do but he repeats the order. 'Lift your tongue! LIFT YOUR TONGUE!'

I prolonged the demonstration and then explained. 'It's only vitamin D. It's not a drug of abuse.'

'Walk away!' was the response. 'WALK AWAY!' Which I did, tossing the rest of my water into a muddy ditch as I left. It was only a little thing but, on a cold day in prison, it doesn't take much.

Only four of the six inmates in my block worked in the laundry. The other two stayed in the unit to run a busy morning of manufacturing and merchandising smokes. Smoking was banned in the prison to protect the health and wellbeing of both inmates and the guards, who were ruled by the same regulations regarding nicotine as other government employees. The prisoners strongly opposed the 'No Smoking' edict, but were unsuccessful – a great blow to many chain smokers. So, necessity is the mother …

Grass from the lawns, or fruit and vegetables, or the lettuce from my salads were initially in high demand – until I got wiser. The grass or food scraps were dried in the microwave or sandwich maker to provide a vehicle to absorb the liquid extracted from soaking used nicotine patches. Wrapped in paper and lit with a spark from batteries, these prison cigarettes were popular, and newbies would be encouraged to go on the patch to ensure a continuing supply. Often in the afternoons, a tired guard's voice would explode from the intercom:

'Will the prisoners on the back lawn please stop picking the grass.'

Business conducted in our quarters when we were at work in the laundry involved other contraband substances smuggled in by visitors (kiss, kiss). Exorbitant costs led to some furious arguments, but it was a busy business involving a constant traffic of highly undesirable individuals in our space and some fairly noxious odours we all tried to ignore.

I was invited into the bathroom one night before lockdown to enjoy a cigarette with the boys. It was a bit rough but the nicotine rush was fun, and they were all amused to see an old man lick a finger and touch it to the side that was burning too fast.

All camaraderie was lost one day when I returned from a hard and fast morning in the laundry to have a coffee in my cell with my feet up. It was the cheapest, nastiest instant coffee around, Continental Roast, peddled in hospitals, nursing homes and prisons around the globe to their uncomplaining clientele. It was always in abundant supply in large tins with bits of clotted sugar left on top. To my horror, I found my limited portion of milk had disappeared from the fridge during the morning's commerce.

'Where's my milk?' I asked the felons gathered at the table.

'It's all gone,' said the main perpetrator, a pugnacious, highly tattooed young man given to loud outbursts and vicious laughter.

'Oh,' I said. 'I hope you had a good morning.'

'There's some other milk there,' he said. 'Someone bought it in when we ran out.'

'Well,' I said, draining a few long-life drops from the container, 'it's run out now,' stomping off to my cell. There was no-one there who cared to defuse the situation and, having left in high dudgeon – although my fellow ruffians would more likely have called it cracking the shits – there was little I could do to calm the situation, which smouldered on until I managed a move to another unit.

EVIL CONJECTURES

Our sandwich maker was confiscated when it was found being used to dry lettuce and grass trimmings. It was no big deal. The consortium still had the microwave. Business went on but highly squashed and burnt sandwiches were off the menu of things to do when you wanted to scream. When the microwave went a few days later for the same reason, business had to move elsewhere.

I was *asked* to share my double cell with a new inmate, a young man coming down from ice; in on a driving charge, but while attempting to evade the police they uncovered a few of his unresolved problems in the past. It was only his second time inside. Before evening lockdown, he had a visit from a very unsavoury customer from a different block who dropped in as a one-man welcoming committee, reassuring him he would soon be transferred to a unit accommodating more of his friends and colleagues. Oh joy!

Once he had slept for most of a week, he was doing circuits of the grounds deep in conversation with various small walking groups. Winter for me, summer camp for others. What a great system!

I was *asked* to share my double cell another time with another young man coming down off ice. Twenty-four and from the wrong side of the tracks, he'd been in the prison before but was having a hard time settling, spending his days in restless sleep. When locked in together he watched TV and dozed. In my diary, I commented on how 'awfully considerate' he was about the two programs I watched, *Antiques Roadshow* and a weekly book club.

I was reading George Eliot one day and writing thank-you letters while his soap TV dialogues were streaming uninvited through my ears. It was an interesting but not impossible exercise to not hear. He asked me what I was reading. I tried to explain the dense but brilliant prose of a mid-nineteenth century radical feminist who outraged society, lived with a married man and published under a male pseudonym. Somehow, it seemed fitting to the radical milieu I found myself in then but my fellow inmate seemed unimpressed. He didn't ask me anything else.

The double cell had been given to me, I felt, in deference to my status as an elderly doctor. Not your usual resident in a prison. No history of violence or antisocial behaviour, respected in the yard as Doc. The spacious cell had a large desk and an expansive – if barred – window facing north across wooded hills, and was often sun-drenched, despite the bitterly cold Tasmanian winter.

Mostly, I had the cell to myself. I laughed when one temporary cellmate, a burglar, moved on and left with my pen, toilet paper and half a packet of dried fruit and nuts. Contrary to common belief, there is no honour amongst thieves.

End of June: Big-screen televisions in the common rooms had short lives, being the most obvious things to destroy on a bad day. Well-behaved units watched movies together after evening lockdown with microwaved popcorn. I couldn't imagine it myself, but then I was invited to join another unit, admittedly by someone in here for a bit of armed robbery, but most of his co-residents were simple marijuana growers. Neat and tidy, they had a fully equipped kitchen with no shortages of milk or breakfast cereals due to drop-ins, and no background bursts of evil laughter. The barracks did, however, turn out to be a major hub in the food and commodity stockpiling and bartering market, which was the basis of a complex financial system, operated by and for the prisoners, which I never fully understood.

13 July 2016: I had a few days away from the laundry due to legal phone calls being booked. When I got back, the manager came up to me to tell me he'd made me full-time and hoped that was OK? How could I disagree? Then he offered me the position of leading hand. It was true that some days the person doing 'leading hand' would get me to give them a hand with cumulative totals. It was fun helping hardened criminals with their maths, seeing them humbled by rows of figures and making light of it for them.

Occasionally workers would come up to me for advice on what to do with unusual items. If feeling off-hand, as I usually was, I would suggest they throw it on the floor and jump up and down on it, which seemed to amuse them before finding someone else to ask. When I was offered the position of leading hand I countered with, 'But I'm leaving soon.' Which garnered roars of laughter from the jolly felons around us.

'You'll never get bail for murd,' they said. 'Forget about it!'

The last thing I wanted was a rise in prisoner status and responsibility in the laundry. When there wasn't enough work in my section, I could wander around chatting and watching other workers at their various stations. The ironing presses were large machines with hot metal sides to lean against. I learned to feed tea towels and pillow cases into the machine faster than they could be folded at the other end, sending the worker there into frenzy until another worker could be co-opted to help. Rather than annoying, it became a standard game in my wanders. Those folding would say, 'Hit me!' as I approached and I would send the ironing through as fast as I could and at odd angles to break it up. Oh, how we laughed! What fun!

Snowing today while calling Jamie from the outside phones.

On cold mornings, the prospect of laundry work sorting hot towels with one slung around my neck was quite comforting. Sometimes a cool breeze would enter through the loading bay, but generally it was a very cosy place to be with a row of ten industrial dryers humming away. During slow times one could lean against the giant, round glass doors to feel the heat.

One particular lively fellow used to dance around the huge machines as he emptied and filled them. In for life for killing his rape victim with a Besser brick, he advised me to forget my life outside and cut all connections with family and friends for my own sanity. Here we have jobs, warm beds, hot meals and an income (a pittance), he would proclaim loudly, while slamming washing machine doors and darting around the laundry. What more do you want? Forget outside, he would say to all the newbies. Give up hope, it sounded like, all who enter here.

No thanks. In charge of the loading and unloading the massive washers and dryers, he would call across the floor to me. 'Doctor D [for Death], Doctor D!' he would loudly hail over the humming of his machines and general chatter.

'Doctor D!' he would call. 'How ya doin' man?'

'Good. Good, Max,' I'd say, or 'Ready for medication Max, double dose.'

Sometimes, he would offer to dispatch me if it got too much and doing time became too onerous. Then he would loudly discuss options and explain which areas of the facility lacked camera surveillance.

'Doctor Death, Doctor Death,' he would start. 'Are you on the boop train yet? Huh? The Boop train, you know. Boop, boop!' I was then informed that this signified buprenorphine, the main contraband available in jail. A long-acting opioid derivative, it came as a powder which, when burned and inhaled, provided up to twenty four hours of release from all pain and distress. Living in paradise.

Often, I would be thrown unusual items that arrived in the hospital laundry to identify. 'A syringe driver holder' or 'it prevents clots forming during knee operations'. Once, I playfully demonstrated good tourniquet application with one of the many that would come through. I showed how to slap the inside of the elbow to get the veins to stand out or 'sit up' before puncture, and other handy measures if this failed. A captive audience formed around me as I went on to explain some simple tricks to avoid bruising. Someone pulled up a bench so everyone could see. It felt mad, but here's to preventative medicine, I thought, as I looked at the gathered faces eager for more.

Ha! Ha! I only did it the once, Your Honour, I imagined myself explaining, and quickly rounded up the tutorial before our benevolent overseer broke us up. Still, they would come to me with odd items found twisted in sheets and say, 'What's this, Doc?'

24 July 2016: I wake from a dream full of villains with murderous intent, thinking, can I sue the police for the corruption of my dream world?

Gave an 'awesome' massage to a man who has just been sentenced to five years (big time, the fine detail was not revealed to me) and he had a laugh that chilled. The same laugh I would hear again and again. A laugh that reeked of lurking evil, a laugh that said it all – and all was not nice, not pleasant or well-intentioned, not warming or heartfelt, not a raucous laugh but a laugh bereft of goodwill or bonhomie. A laugh that is cold and cruel, half-snarl, a pirate's laugh: callous, braying, nasty, false, forced and hollow. A laugh that would cause mothers to unconsciously gather the young ones to their skirts and hold the babies closer, to wrap their shawls tighter around their shoulders.

I can't begrudge the bluster, but the diabolical laughter heard over and over wherever men congregated was chilling. Now, when I hear bursts of it here, on the outside, I freeze and turn my head slowly, looking for evil.

23 July 2016: After two days of dejection since the postponement of a bail hearing and a day and night of severe neck pain with a cervicogenic headache no doubt prompted by the dejection, it was eventually relieved by (listen to the drum roll) prayer. I had a catharsis of sorts and afterwards spent an evening with the boys playing gangland shoot-ups on the big screen, followed by some macho group exercise and then some blackhead removals. Hey, Dad, look at me, hanging out with the criminal element! I got through the evening smiling all the way.

We have two brothers in at the moment, both here for armed robbery of a pharmacy. Seemingly nice young lads, no evil chuckling, we've spent some pleasant time discussing their favourite varieties of opiates and the newer synthetic varieties. They described fascinating techniques in bypassing the various pharmacological additives designed as deterrents to converting oral varieties for intravenous use.

The seemingly sensible and supposedly foolproof methods used by the pharmaceutical companies were revealed to me as mere time-consuming hurdles on the way to producing drug forms suitable for the intravenous explosion of enjoyment of the poppies' ancient and powerful pacifying properties. Who was I to argue? It clearly wasn't the time or place to discuss harm-minimisation or the latest narcotic-withdrawal techniques. Sometimes, it felt like I was in first-year criminal university, still undecided about my specialty, although I do enjoy a good burn. I'm quite fond of a beer and a bonfire …

Waiting in a queue for the phone. There are only two for 280 residents, outdoors with little cover from wind and swirling rain. Once or twice, it snowed. This day, I was waiting with only an hour left before evening lockdown. Calls cut out at five minutes and there were quite a few people milling around, maybe six with a few others in a holding pattern walking circuits and reminding all of their place in the queue each time they passed.

A shady character arrived with neck and jaw tatts and a set of roman numerals over one eyebrow. He asked about the queue and was not quiet about his dissatisfaction. I was next in line for one of the phones, a regular crim waiting for the other. So the new arrival chose me to demonstrate a variety of standover techniques, to which I showed some resistance until my father's words, any father's words, came to me: choose your battles carefully son and don't start one you'll probably lose.

No-one gave me cheek for walking away from an ex-boxing champion, a frequent flyer and a 'heavy dude'. Watching from a distance, I could see the nature of his phone call was unsavoury in the extreme. Spitting as he snarled and punching the brick wall for emphasis, with all the expletives removed from the exchange it would have been very, very short.

Despite our quibbles over food distribution, here's a heartwarming story of unit cohesion. The word came down about a man about to join our crew. Max was a recidivist. Well-known to the old hands, he was considered mad and violent. Don't let him get you alone, was the warning.

After being escorted by the guards to his cell, Max refused to come out for a chat until it was time for a crap, when he got *bumped* in the bathroom (out of camera range) and the guards were called. An unfortunate fall. He was quickly transferred to the prison hospital. Multiple fractures, we heard next day, a very bad fall, but we all felt safe that night, tucked in by one of our top toughs. It was suggested that Max was sent to our block for just that reason, but that may have been a boast or part of our flattering thanks.

26 July 2016: Finally, after three months, the day arrived when I got back in that tin box in a bus and was driven down the river, over the bridge and into the barred basement of the Supreme Court. After appearing briefly before the judge, I waited in a holding cell for his lunch to settle and time for deliberation. My pacing area was much reduced but after four hours I was again conducted upstairs and granted bail.

In deference to my laundry felons, I am only the second person in Australia's legal history to get bail for murder. Looking through the notes I made in prison was confronting. Revisiting all the anguish was difficult but the pages of outrage also revealed me to myself as a bit of a pompous git. I am amazed in retrospect that I didn't score at least one black eye. I guess my age, my glasses and my readiness to act the part of the mad doctor, making crazy faces on demand as I walked the grounds, saved me from harm.

And now, four years later, lying in a large hot bath, I wonder how long I will remember those animal howls of the mentally deranged who have met with another crisis and have been again incarcerated. It is the knee-jerk reaction of a bad parent. Even the most vicious recidivist could be given a piece of garden to work as their own. Give them some dignity and purpose before the hopeless tatts creep up over the chin! By this I mean visible tattoos on neck or hands. Called *job stoppers* when they encroach onto the face, they are usually the art of lifers. Some of the tattooed faces passed in corridors were both grotesque and frightening but rarely seen outside.

Looking back, incarceration was not a horror of Dickensian proportions. The cells were neither damp nor cold, though getting an extra pillow required some cunning. The vegetarian food was consistently awful but not inedible. It was the daily dehumanisation which seemed to lag so far behind the intellectual progress of our society. The continued imprisonment of the mentally deranged is itself clearly insane.

What happened to rehabilitation and retraining, of workshop skills, car repairs, apprenticeships? Expanding in-prison services beyond hospital laundry? Meaningful work, prison farms to provide food, agricultural and kitchen training? It seems so ridiculously simple to reform the expensive enterprise of state prisons we are all paying for.

If incarceration continues as the ongoing solution for all the too-hard-basket cases, could we at least get ahead of overcrowding and understaffing in our only jail and clear the two-to-four-year backlog of on-remand cases in prison waiting to be heard in Tasmania, the longest delay of all the states and territories of Australia. How do these supposedly innocent people feel? How does the jail culture treat them?

By a process of elimination, I suppose, prison guards tend towards a level of coarseness. The enjoyment many of them show when called upon to enforce the subjugation of their charges was always disgusting to watch.

I got to know a few of the guards. One I would see on escort duty, moving to and from medical appointments or visitors. He was a burnt-out paramedic. He knew my story and would ask how my case and I were going in a way I would want to answer.

The other was an Amazon, a basketball player recently arrived on the job. Working in the general crew, she was a breath of fresh air; well-meaning, eager to help, willing to calm rather than stoke our angst, she stood out as someone who was not yet callous. I can't remember where she came from but I urged her to leave for a better-paid job in security before she developed body graffiti and an evil laugh.

That was two, but what about the rest? Tattoos, gym-pumped and vicious. Goes with the job. WHY? Reforms stymied by stubborn intransigence. WHY? I saw guards in the suicide-risk barracks incite violent outbursts and then take delight in overcoming any resistance to their might; other guards joining in if backup was required, reminiscent of a team sport. As I have said, it was truly disgusting practice and we fellow inmates would be forced to look away or be drawn into the shouted abuse. Is this what we have become? Where is the independent oversight, the inmate feedback?

There is none. Although there have been countless inquiries and recommendations on how to run a prison, I watched trained guards routinely baiting mentally challenged people like animals in a cage. How sick is that?

The symbology of prison tatts was not something I explored inside, but it was pretty clear that when they spread up the neck and onto the face, it was the face of a lifer or someone who had spent a very large part of their lives behind bars, mostly high-security bars.

We didn't see a lot of them in medium security. They were a breed apart, often seen with more than one escort in the corridors. You do see them out of jail sometimes, at petrol stations or in a queue at a take-out counter with maybe a black beanie over a crew cut and wraparound mirrored sunglasses.

'Walk on!' says a voice in my head. 'Do not make eye contact! Move on!'

But when they turn and say, 'Hey, Doc, how are you?' what can I say …?

The question people don't ask about my time in jail is this. Did it change you?

The answer is yes. Oh yes. Yes. YES.

But how?

Don't fuckin' ask!

CHAPTER FIVE: BAIL

PUBLISHED TO THE PARTIES ONLY UNTIL FURTHER NOTICE

File Nos 1370/2016, 145/2016

STEPHEN JOHN EDWARDS v STATE OF TASMANIA

REASONS FOR JUDGMENT ESTCOURT J

26 July 2016

1 The applicant, Stephen John Edwards, is a 61-year-old medical practitioner without any relevant prior convictions. He has been charged with the murder of his 88-year-old mother who died, it is alleged, of drug toxicity at about 8.30pm on 4 March 2016.

2 On the State's case the applicant murdered his mother by the administration of medication (in particular, morphine and midazolam) in circumstances where her various medical conditions were not imminently fatal and such palliation as was administered was not appropriate.

3 The State asserts that the applicant is guilty of murder on the basis of either s 157(1)(a) or s 157(1)(c) of the Criminal Code in that, either he unilaterally decided that his mother wished to commit suicide in accordance with her long expressed wish

to die with her co-dependent husband of 68 years who had died on 2 March 2016 or, alternatively, that he was reckless in administering to his mother drugs that had been prescribed for his father by his father's general practitioner Dr Smith.

157. Cases in which culpable homicide is murder

(1) Culpable homicide is murder if it is committed –

(a) with an intention to cause the death of any person, whether of the person killed or not;

(b) with an intention to cause to any person, whether the person killed or not, bodily harm which the offender knew to be likely to cause death in the circumstances, although he had no wish to cause death;

(c) by means of any unlawful act or omission which the offender knew, or ought to have known, to be likely to cause death in the circumstances, although he had no wish to cause death or bodily harm to any person;

4 The applicant, himself a palliative care and aged care practitioner, denies that he intended to kill his mother and claims that he initially administered her own medication, clonazepam, a sleeping drug, to her because she wished to sleep, and that he later administered morphine and midazolam only after his mother developed Cheyne-Stokes breathing, was near death and would by that time have developed brain damage.

5 About two weeks prior to her death, the applicant's mother and his father had made a pact to kill themselves following the unexpected death of one of their sons in Thailand. They refused to eat or drink, and dehydration ensued, and ultimately led to the death of the applicant's father who also suffered advanced and imminently fatal lymphoma and was palliated by the applicant.

6 The State contends that the applicant may also have murdered his father and asserts that provides an additional reason why he might abscond if granted bail. The proposition that the applicant recklessly administered morphine and midazolam to his father is not supported by the evidence of the State Pathologist, Dr Ritchey, as to Mr Edward's death which is before me on this application. Moreover, Mr Edward's death certificate was signed by his general practitioner Dr Smith who had prescribed the palliation medication in the first place and attended after Mr Edward's death.

7 I will consider the possibility that an added incentive for the applicant to abscond could be that another charge of murder might be brought against him in the event that Dr Ritchey changed his view as to the innocent circumstances of Mr Edward's death, or if someone else expressed an expert opinion contrary to Dr Ritchey's view. However, on the material I have I do not rate the impact of such a likelihood on the applicant as significant. That is the only relevance of the State's assertion in my view.

8 As far as the strength of the State's case is concerned, an assertion that the applicant murdered his father could not be evidence on his trial for the murder of his mother. It could only amount to tendency or coincidence evidence if it could be proved as a fact and if it could be so proved then the State would of necessity have already charged the applicant with his father's murder.

9 Returning to the case against the applicant as to the murder of his mother, the State asserts that the applicant told police at the time of his mother's death and before he returned to NSW where he lived, that his mother 'no longer wanted to be here' and that she probably had renal failure and suffered from dementia and hypertension, but did not mention the

drugs he administered to her. The relevance of that may or may not be significant. Mrs Edwards had been on a two-week hunger strike – the applicant may well have thought that renal failure was the cause of death. That he did not mention the drugs could have been as a result of the nature and extent of the police officer's inquiries of him.

10 The State also submits that it adds colour to its case that the applicant took the clonazepam back to Sydney with him. That is not something that necessarily sheds any light on the strength of the State's case. The applicant is an aged care doctor and will contend that drug was useful in his practice. And, I note, he did not remove the leftover morphine in a similar way as one might think he would if he had acted criminally or was intending in the future to so act using powerful drugs.

11 The State also says that the applicant's brother, Robert, made a statement that he did not believe that his mother committed suicide. He may well think that. However, that does not establish a unilateral decision on the part of the applicant that his mother wished to commit suicide.

12 The State also says that in his record of interview with police the applicant used the word 'robust' to describe his mother's health. That may be but I am told that the record of interview is 100 pages long and that the applicant apparently also told police that his mother had not taken food or water for a couple of weeks and that she was dehydrated. I am also told that he said that he did not intend to kill his mother and that he only administered the morphine and midazolam after she developed Cheyne-Stokes breathing – that is end stage breathing after the administration of the clonazepam.

13 If all of that is established, and it is by no means fanciful, the applicant would be entitled to a verdict of not guilty of

any crime. Palliation to ease the imminent and inevitable death of a person by depressing the central nervous system, so long as it is not intended to be in itself inevitably fatal, is accepted as valid medical treatment as I understand Professor Odell's report.

14 Finally, the State suggests that it is relevant that the applicant did not call his mother's GP to attend after her death. It transpires however that the doctor who did attend was the 'on-call' doctor for Dr Smith's after hours' practice. It is unsurprising that the on-call doctor would not sign the death certificate. Mrs Edwards was not his patient and he was not in attendance at her death.

15 The applicant submits that at its highest the case against him will be that he assisted his ill mother to die in accordance with her long-expressed wish to die with her co-dependent husband of 68 years.

16 The applicant's mother was a retired maternity nurse who had made an enduring power of attorney in March 2003 in favour of her son David. In that power of attorney she had required her guardian to observe, among other things, that he was to confer with the applicant in all matters relating to her health and welfare, that she believed in euthanasia and that she did not wish any steps to be taken to prolong her life or to receive any unnecessary palliative care.

17 The State relies for the strength of its case on the opinion of Professor Morris Odell

(Victorian Institute of Forensic Medicine; Head, Clinical Forensic Medicine Services, Morris Odell BE (Hons) MBBS FRACGP DMJ FACLM FFFLM)

who is of the view that there was no justification in the medical record for the high doses of morphine and benzodiazepines that were administered to Mrs Edwards by the applicant on the day of her death.

18 The State Forensic Pathologist, Dr Ritchey, on the other hand has stated that 'this complex case presents several possibilities with regard to cause of death'. The possibilities he raises are the advanced natural disease of the heart and blood vessels, the possibility of small vessel thrombosis and ischemia resulting in fatal cardiac arrhythmia, peri-mortem seizure (on a history of head injury-induced seizures) and mixed drug toxicity, specifically the combination of morphine and midazolam, by central nervous system depression and respiratory arrest.

19 The applicant's mother suffered dehydration in addition to multiple health problems including (malignant hypertension, myelodysplasia, osteoporosis, chronic back pain, cardiovascular disease, senile cardiac amyloidosis, chronic subdural haematoma, history of multiple falls, post-traumatic seizures and vascular dementia with significant decline in mobility and cognition.

20 In respect of drug toxicity, whilst Dr Ritchey opines that it is a likely cause of death, he concedes that several or all of the factors may have contributed to Mrs Edward's death by their combined effects.

21 The State's case may be strong viewed solely on the basis of Professor Odell's opinion or read in conjunction with Dr Ritchey's report but Dr Ritchey's report admits of doubt, and it is obvious that there will be much argument about the medical evidence in what Dr Ritchey describes as 'a complex case'.

22 The case will no doubt involve expert evidence in the fields of toxicology, pathology and palliative care.

23 The fundamental question to be determined on any application for bail is whether or not the applicant will appear to answer bail if it is granted; R v Fisher (1964) 14 Tas R 12 at 13 per Crawford J (Snr).

24 The nature of the offence charged, the severity of the possible sentence and the strength of the State's case are said to be additional considerations, but, properly regarded, they are only matters that are relevant to the central question of whether the applicant will answer bail.

25 Prima facie every accused person is entitled to their freedom until trial. No one should be punished by imprisonment before conviction. To place too much reliance on the strength of the State's case is to prejudge the matter.

26 The safety and security of members of the public is a matter to be taken into account, but notwithstanding the veiled suggestion concerning the applicant's removal of clonazepam tablets, I do not see any threat to the public in this case. In any event, the applicant is not presently entitled to practise medicine.

27 Special considerations apply to persons who allegedly have committed offences while on bail. That is not the case here.

28 However, murder is a special case. As submitted on behalf of the applicant, the common law rules provide that bail will only be granted on a charge of murder if the applicant shows 'special or unusual circumstances' or 'exceptional circumstances', or 'extremely exceptional circumstances', or is a 'rare case that is sufficiently exceptional'.

29 There does not seem to be any relevant distinction between those expressions when the facts of the cited cases and the outcomes are examined. See Re a Bail Application [1966] VR 506; R v Hughes [1983] Qd R 92 at 94; Lim v Gregson [1989] WAR I at 13 and 32; Mercanti v WA [2005] WASCA 254 at [17], [44] and [45]; Milenkovski v WA [2011] WASCA 99 at [21], [28], [35], [50] and [51]; Re an Application for bail by Costa [2013] ACTSC 15 at [2]-[4].

30 In State of Tasmania v Neill-Fraser, an unreported decision of Blow J (as he then was) of 20 November 2009, his Honour adopted the statement of principles in cases such as the present, as set out by Crawford J (as he then was) in Smith v Bonde, another unreported decision of 17 December 2001. In that latter case Crawford J said at [2]:

'There is a prima facie rule that every person is entitled to his freedom until trial and the major consideration on a bail application is usually whether he will answer his bail and appear at trial. However, in a case of murder it has frequently been said by courts that the circumstances must be extremely exceptional before bail will be granted and the applicant bears the onus of showing that the circumstances are such that he should be released on bail. See for example Lim v Gregson [1989] WAR 1. The primary reason why exceptional circumstances must be shown before bail is granted to a person charged with murder is that there is a far greater likelihood that he will abscond than in the case of an offender who faces a less serious charge. That was particularly so when a sentence of death or life imprisonment was an inevitable consequence of conviction. Now that criminal courts have power to impose a finite term of imprisonment the argument against granting bail in a murder is not quite as strong, but nevertheless the principle requiring exceptional circumstances still applies.'

31 However, while it can no longer be said that a grant of bail on the charge of murder is very unusual, stringent conditions are often applied as for example in R v Hal/as (2001) 81 SASR 1, where electronic monitoring was a condition of bail. See also Smith v Bonde where two cash sureties each of $40,000 were required, one from a family member and one from a non-family member. I note that Lim v Gregson (above) was a case very similar to the present where bail was granted on such conditions as would provide adequate safeguards to ensure the applicant's attendance at trial.

32 I do not regard the applicant as a flight risk at all. He did not oppose his extradition to Tasmania from New South Wales, where he ordinarily lives, and to where he returned in the ordinary course of events. He has no relevant prior convictions. He is of good character as attested by at least one medical referee whose reference I have read, and he is regarded by that referee as a principled person. The State does not assert otherwise. The applicant has family ties in Tasmania.

33 Moreover, I would expect that the facts of the case are such that the applicant would welcome the opportunity to justify his actions, and if justified return to the practise of his profession. I see no realistic prospect that the applicant would flee, and in such a case one must question the utility of a surety or the deposit of a cash sum in Court. If the applicant, despite my assessment, decided to leave the country, neither a surety nor a cash deposit would prevent him. In any event in the context of the modern world a fugitive would be unlikely to get far if his or her passport were required to be surrendered.

34 There is likely to be a significant delay before trial. The preliminary proceedings are, I am told, likely to take at least

three days and are unlikely to be heard until late September. They may be adjourned. There may be further delay as a result of the State and the defence obtaining further expert opinions.

35 The trial is, in my view, unlikely to be heard until this time next year or later. The applicant has already been in custody for three months and the State is still gathering evidence. I accept that is not of itself a sufficient reason to grant bail, but it is a circumstance that is relevant in the overall aggregation of circumstances to be examined for their qualification as exceptional.

36 Equally, this is not a case where there is any likelihood that the applicant would interfere with the evidence, or would intimidate or suborn witnesses or hinder police inquiries.

37 I am informed that the applicant has not resisted the Medical Board of Australia's suspension of his medical registration, and he has no intention of seeking to practise medicine until the proceedings relating to the charge against him are finalised. I have already said that I do not see any prospect that the safety and the security of the public is at risk.

38 I also accept that given present arrangements at Risdon Prison as to available days and times for accused persons to confer with their legal representatives, the applicant would be hampered in preparation of his defence in such a complex case should he remain in custody. It would be more difficult for him to give instructions, and he would not be able to see his solicitor and counsel as often as he would wish or as may be necessary. As I have said, this is a complex medical case and the applicant's own input into the preparation of the defence would be important, given that he is a medical practitioner, and given that he has, it

seems, significant experience in the area of medicine from which expert opinion evidence will be drawn.

39 In view of the considerations I have enumerated I am satisfied that exceptional circumstances have been shown in this case and that it is appropriate to grant bail. I will hear counsel as to the appropriate conditions of bail.

—

While I was languishing at Her Majesty's pleasure, the prosecution and defence teams had been garnishing expert opinions for and against me. These are discussed later, but how do I now describe those intervening years between release from prison until the charges were dropped? I gather pen and paper and bare my body to the autumn sun in a harbourside park. Always lean, I've lost a quarter of my weight in the last twelve months since my cancer diagnosis. With a few beers to fortify myself against the public gaze and at a distance where my stick-like limbs are less likely to scare small children, I watch families promenading with prams, and dogs scampering along happily.

The sun and the beer relax me. I don't want to think about the recent past. Men are proficient at hiding things away, stuffing unpleasant memories deep in drawers at the back of the mind. 'How are you mate?' 'Fine, fine. How are the kids?'

How to convey the drawn-out anguish of waiting, hoping, waiting for the case to resolve? Waiting to explain myself. I can't Google myself for fear of the false reporting out there. Better to drink beer and forget. 'Keep your head down,' the lawyers cautioned. 'Enjoy the time you have left.'

Well, I've escaped Tasmania and a poisonous relationship. I live in a sunny studio in Elizabeth Bay, Sydney, furnished with the last of a windfall superannuation payment and augmented with side tables and table lamps retrieved from the street.

I live modestly now, polishing stories written over the years and writing this one, wondering if the cancer will give me the time to finish its telling. When people ask, I call myself a writer and a retired doctor. And a harpist.

After working on a few pieces and armed with a busking permit, I played with gusto one evening in a long, echoing pedestrian tunnel in the city full of busy commuters. It was to prove to myself that I was capable of playing for my supper. My cap soon filled with coins. It had been a dream of mine to one day be proficient enough to busk around Europe and South America. Now I'm ready.

Back to the story. My relief on getting bail was, of course, immense. I was released into the surety of a friend whom I'll call Sonya. Sonya lived in a small house with no close neighbours in a remote country area an hour or so from Hobart. Freedom! There, I was happy to isolate, still thinking a trial and vindication were close at hand. I sat feeding a slow-combustion heater and drinking beer. I spoke to my partner, still in Woy Woy, every day.

There was still an expectation that the case would be soon resolved. Battle lines were drawn before my release from jail. The Crown had reports from the coroner and a palliative care specialist. The defence had a pathologist who questioned the conclusions drawn by the coroner, suggesting my mother's death was due to multiple factors other than the drugs given, and the drug levels defined were open to question. The toxicology report was full of provisos regarding the interpretation of the drug levels found that could easily be discredited as not without doubt in the courtroom. A palliative care physician supported my use of medication and at the doses detailed. A geriatrician advised that, although the treatment of family members by a doctor was ill-advised due to issues of clouded judgement, that in exceptional circumstances it was not inappropriate.

These reports are all considered more closely in the next chapter, but my understanding was that in a circumstantial case – no witnesses, no confession, no direct link between the accused and the cause or method of death – the accused cannot be convicted if a reasonable alternative hypothesis is available – i.e., in my case, that my mother died of natural causes. Her time had come.

It is the role of the prosecution to present the evidence to the jury leaving no room for doubt. If doubt exists in the jury's mind, they must acquit. The judge includes this instruction during his final directions.

My mother was dying. There was no proof that any intervention from me directly caused her actual demise. Bring it on, I thought. My team seemed to think we had a good chance and the prosecution case was weak but, despite continued directions hearings, the case dragged on. The prosecution kept stalling. Investigations were ongoing. After more and more delays, the judges tried to apply pressure, but still the vague response of 'ongoing investigations' continued from the prosecution. How could a murder be still under investigation four years after the death?

Money was running out. It was time to sell our beautiful house and get my partner down from NSW, as a quick resolution of the case became more and more remote. The first directions hearing was not until a long eight months after I left prison. The police wanted more time.

Thirteen more times I went to court for directions hearings between 6 March 2017 and 5 August 2019. Thirteen times I expected the case to move to trial. After the last hearing it was still another eight months before the charges were dropped on medical grounds. Why?

Before I introduce the disgruntled niece with the gossip and rumour that complicated the case, I should explain myself. And rather than labour through that, it would be easier to reprint a letter I struggled over after my mother had died and before my arrest for her murder. A letter I wrote to an imaginary medical court or coroner detailing my experience and thinking; a letter I mentioned in conversation with my partner while in prison that I hoped would vindicate me; a letter outlining my experience with medically assisted dying in cases of existential distress. It was a copy of this letter which the Tasmanian Police went back to Woy Woy to pursue but never found, a letter left sitting on my hard drive, which the police picked up on their first visit to New South Wales on my behalf.

CHAPTER SIX:
TO THE CORONER

Re: the demise of Nelda Edwards 27/2/1928 – 4/3/2016

I arrived in Hobart from Woy Woy in NSW on 1/3/2016 to be with and assist in the imminent demise of my father David Edwards, a ninety-year-old man with atrial fibrillation, locally advanced prostate cancer and moderate dementia. His energy and mobility had been deteriorating rapidly in the previous two months, the onset of which I had noted on my last visit before Christmas when the progression of his dementia was also apparent. Since being informed on 25/3/2016 of their second son's unexpected and unexplained death in Thailand only five days earlier, they were both grief-stricken and decided to stop eating and drinking as a means to ending their own lives.

Both my parents had expressed their wish many times for many years to all four sons and sisters-in-law that when the time came they wished to actively die together using whatever means available before debility and loss of dignity occurred. My mother had me promise as a 19-year-old nursing student to end her life if she developed dementia, a condition she has had for at least the last eight years. She had joked in the past with her first son's wife that if demented, she wanted to be hit on the head with a rolling pin. My mother had also many times within her family expressed a wish to die before if not with my father and not to survive after his demise.

My arrival was prompted by my younger brother's phone call advising me that he could see my father's teeth through his cheeks, which I interpreted as severe wasting and dehydration. I arranged a flight the next day and called the local GP informing him of my father's decline and my intention to be at his bedside and assist with his passing. I requested scripts for oral morphine and clonazepam drops to be collected by my younger brother. I rang the chemist to check supply and the drops were ordered to arrive at midday the following day.

When I arrived at 10 am it was clear my father was indeed dehydrated, extremely weak, drowsy and bed-bound. He complained of mild ache in a hip due to a fall on 24 February 2016 due to difficulty standing from a deep armchair. His sit-to-stand ability bad been increasingly poor for a few weeks prior to cessation of food and fluid. An ambulance had been called subsequent to my mother's personal alarm being activated a few weeks earlier. My father had fallen to the floor and was unable to get up even with his wife's aid. The officers assisted my father to bed but both my parents adamantly refused his transfer to hospital. Despite repeated suggestions for years by myself and my brothers for a move to safer assisted-living arrangements or cohabitation with one of their sons, my parents were always resolute in their wish to live together independently in their own home until removed in wooden boxes.

I gave my father a small dose of oral morphine syrup to ease his pain and distress when I arrived. Then I went to introduce myself to the local GP and collect some clonazepam drops that weren't available earlier. The GP Dr Johnny Smith was very helpful. My younger brother had brought both my parents to see him on 24/2/2016 prior to the fall because my father was suffering from constipation and difficulty voiding. I explained my expertise in aged and palliative care and requested further scripts for morphine and midazolam as if-required subcutaneous administration for an anticipated home death. I had worked in the same practice as a GP for a period of 12 to 18 months five years previously when living in Hobart, so the staff were also congenial and gave me the needles and syringes necessary. The local chemist provided the drops, ampoules, some lip balm and the address of a medical supplier for a Kylie, or waterproof under sheet, I returned to the house and administered a small dose of clonazepam to my now delirious and semi-conscious father to help him settle.

Once my father was asleep my mother asked why she too was not dying, as they had both been fasting for the same time. I explained that she was comparatively robust and was not dying and so I could not assist with her request for similar sedation. She became distraught and hugged my father, begging him to return to her.

He did not regain consciousness. My mother shared the bed with him that night and in the morning noted restlessness and asked me to give him something to help him settle. I gave him three subcutaneous doses of morphine and midazolam through the morning at half-hourly-to-hourly intervals as his breathing became increasingly stertorous. He died at 10.10 am.

Although grief-stricken and determined not to eat and drink, my mother had agreed after my arrival to recommence her medications from a Webster-pak which included three antihypertensives; candesartan 32mg, lercanidipine 10mg mane and metoprolol 100mg BD. Her blood pressure was raised: 180/120, which increased the risk of a further transient ischaemic attack or worse, a debilitating stroke which would require institutional care, a fact more distressing to her than taking the tablets.

Subsequent to my father's death I spent much time with my mother encouraging her to consider recommencing food and drink and the possibility of moving in with one of her remaining three sons. My mother's resolve to live alone and to not eat or drink was unshakable. Her resolve to join her husband seemed hardened by grief. All the food had been discarded from their fridge after my parents discovered their son in Thailand had been found dead.

My mother was a keen and talented cook but the progression of her dementia meant that she had arrived at the burn-pot point some two years previously. A fall eighteen months previously led to a subdural haemorrhage requiring burr holes to relieve intercranial pressure and a slow return to consciousness. The resultant acquired brain injury prevented her continuing her principal pastime of cross-stitch. Her previously meticulous copperplate handwriting became a wavering scrawl. Her mobility was extremely poor and her impulsiveness required continual supervision and prompting to use a four-wheel walker; however, with ongoing physiotherapy, daily physical exercises, writing practice and word-finding puzzles, she had made a remarkable recovery but was still dependent on her husband to provide breakfast and the evening meals. Although extremely irritated when her sons insisted on her husband surrendering his driver's licence two years previously, the pair still managed with taxis to enjoy lunch out daily, albeit with increasingly bird-like portion sizes. As my father's strength and mobility declined, his increasing difficulty opening doors and pulling in a chair to the table had terminated this habit a few months ago. Their co-dependance was heart-rending. My younger brother, recently retired, spent more and more time taking them to lunch, medical appointments and helping my father through the supermarket until frailty forced him to stay in the car while my brother struggled to interpret increasingly illegible shopping lists.

After my father's death my mother was even more determined not to eat or drink. She took her medications knowing the included sedation would help her chronic insomnia. I assured her the remaining week-and-a-half of medication packaging did not include enough Serepax 15mg tablets to constitute an overdose and my father's oral morphine and clonazepam drops were never left in their bedroom and were, from then, hidden.

I hoped for a change of mind. My mother made a show of accepting a once savoured brandy and dry but only took a few sips. My eldest brother and his wife arrived post-haste from a holiday in Victoria, too late for our father's death but able to console my mother somewhat through the rest of the day and the day following. Dismayed by the procession of conciliatory friends and relatives, our mother took to her bed at 5 pm. The elder brother, also a poor sleeper, quietly got into her bed at 5.30 the next morning to hold her and slumber with her until she awoke. She was delighted on waking, thinking it had been her husband beside her.

As we sat around the bed with her, she calmly explained she knew how to cut her wrists but didn't want to be found in a cold and bloody bath. She wanted to sleep. She wanted to join her husband in heaven and see her dead son smiling. She didn't want me to get into any trouble but their intention to get the required 'Dr Nitschke tablets' had never been fulfilled. She may have slept well because of extra Serepax.

Now, I do have experience with legal terminal sedation in three cases in what it was termed existential distress. In 2001, I worked for a year as a registrar with the Sydney Institute of

Palliative Medicine working in hospices and in the community with palliative care nurses in assisting home death. I cared for a thirty-five-year-old man with a hugely distended abdomen from renal cancer who always demanded a quick exit when his time came. When his symptoms eventually became unmanageable in his home he went into a nearby hospice and asked my superiors for permission to begin sedation. There were arguments but the patient was adamant. Eventually the sedation was given. He woke 12 hours later, furious to be still alive and stormed outside for a cigarette. He then climbed back into bed and received a second dose from which he didn't wake.

A few years ago, I was working in Huonville. It was purpose built, spacious and well maintained. Most of the residents and staff came from the surrounding hills. The Nursing Unit Manager was also a local whose father I helped her care for until his death at home. In the three years I worked there I became responsible for half the patients in a 100-bed aged-care facility facing the river in Franklin. I had a proud patient diagnosed with breast cancer which had metastised to bone and brain. She refused treatment but then acquiesced to the wishes of her children. Wearing a scratchy wig over her remaining wispy hair, she came to see me one day, still well-dressed and walking erect, demanding a trial of my 'nice nursing home'. On arrival she promptly drew the curtains in her room across the expansive view of river and hills beyond, pulled off her wig, insisted on eating alone and resisted all our attempts to integrate her into the life of the home.

After checking a few times for the possible onset of early morning headache or blurred vision, she announced she had had enough. She did not want to wait for the development of symptoms or the loss of word-finding puzzle ability, her only pastime. She wanted her gradual decline to be over and, despite our protests that she was comfortable and not losing weight, she was adamant in her resolve to have her life ended. I rang the palliative care doctor in Hobart. He was unsympathetic. I was advised to trial an antidepressant. A week later it had made no difference and, despite the insufficient time for an adequate trial, her requests for an early end persisted. I rang the palliative care doctor. Again, he was unhelpful. I asked to speak to the professor, his superior. When I detailed the case he said, 'Call the family! I will be there in the morning.'

Gathered in her room, the professor asked her to state her case, which she did calmly and succinctly. Then he asked the daughters and husband to say how they felt. The daughters wept and pleaded with their mother to come to one of their homes, all nearby, so they could support and care for her. The husband, tears silently rolling down his cheeks, added he didn't want her to die but if that was her wish, so be it. The professor then said to the old woman you may have your wish. Once the director of nursing had reassured a few reluctant nurses with metaphors of putting farm animals out of their miseries, the sedation began. Again, she woke once. Again, we gave another dose. She returned to a sleep from which she didn't wake.

The third time I suggested the existential distress clause was appropriate was with a youngish man from Cygnet who had slipped in goose poo and broken his neck, only to discover he had extensive bone metastases from an unknown primary. A well-known local character who lived alone in a self-constructed humpy deep in the hills behind the town, he couldn't leave a party without several curtain calls, telling everyone who listened that when his time came he would 'take himself out'.

The local vet politely declined to help. His friends threw a gun he had procured into the river. When that time approached, he entered the palliative care unit in Hobart but so irritated the staff there with his continual demands for a medicated end and then requests for just another day that he was eventually sent to the nursing home in Franklin in which I worked as a hopeless case. His pleas for sedation followed by further pleas for yet another day to complete his journal continued. The palliative care physicians in Hobart were again unsympathetic.

Slowly he lost weight. With an increasingly faint voice he continued to plead and then again, would vacillate. Under pressure from his distressed mother, I persisted in pleading on his behalf to the palliative care team in Hobart. Eventually permission was granted and the patient was ready. The nurses were all on-board. He was, by then, very close to death. It didn't take long.

The last case in which I tried to use the clause of existential distress was that of an elderly widow, just a few years ago, who came under my care in Woy Woy where I was managing about one hundred and fifty hostel and nursing home residents. Her name was Joyce. She had lung cancer and had managed to live at home for a few years with the help of supplemental oxygen until the tumour had replaced most of one lung. After some time in the local hospital her condition had become hopeless and she was transferred to the nursing home to die.

She had trouble sleeping with the standard medications until I gave her clonazepam. She was so grateful. Exhausted by the struggle to breathe each day, sleep was her only relief. She asked me to help her sleep more. From a humble woman it was a very tactful request. I spoke to the local palliative care doctor who rudely refused to see her or have anything to do with the case. I was asking for euthanasia, he said, and if I hastened her death and it came to court he would not support me.

I asked a female doctor on the same team, hoping for a more compassionate response, and, though after some pleading, she did visit; she criticised aspects of the nursing care and again refused my request for terminal sedation. Having highlighted her case, I could not then surreptitiously ease her out gently with morphine. I did what I could to alleviate the oxygen hunger but her children, the nurses and I had to watch her anguish and wait another long month for her suffering to inevitably come to an end. When I asked another doctor who cared for people in the same facility what they would have done they said, don't ask, just do what needs to be done. It was a hard lesson for me but a lot harder for the patient.

My mother was also a very proud woman from the country. When she was fourteen years old her horse on the homeward gallop ran into an extra clothesline that had been strung across the path. Most of my mother's teeth were knocked out. We never saw her without her dentures. She slept with them in. Before a hip replacement after a fall in her garden the anaesthetist asked her if she had her own teeth.

'Yes,' she declared. After the operation the surgeon challenged her over the dentures. 'But they *are* mine,' she insisted.

She once confided in me that my father had never seen her out of her nightie. She would have been appalled by nursing assistance with showering. She had kept a spotless house and resented the care-package cleaning after the fall but appreciated the help in her garden after an earlier crush fracture in her lower back moving a large pot of orchids rendered her gait lopsided with a pronounced stoop she would straighten from whenever visitors arrived.

I didn't fancy another argument with the palliative care service. My mother would have hated the assessment with strangers in and out of her bedroom. My parents have always been very private, don't-make-a-fuss people. I succumbed. Who needs to know? At 8.30 am I gave her a decent dose of clonazepam: 2.5 mg. Propped up by pillows, she waited. Half an hour later I gave her another dose.

She became drowsy. Half an hour later I give her another dose. She fell into a light sleep but half an hour later was awake again. Despairing. I gave her another dose along with 10 mg of morphine syrup, praying for a synergistic effect. It worked. She slept.

My elder brother and I stayed by the bed. Occasionally she would murmur something and change position but as the day progressed she became more still. My younger brother, shocked by the sight of her dentures falling loosely in her mouth, stayed with the wives in the kitchen. Aghast but unable to leave her side, my older brother asked me what would happen and I told him she would probably wake again when the medications wore off but by 4 pm her breathing became irregular.

Knowing death was approaching, I gave a single subcutaneous dose of morphine and midazolam. Slowly the gaps in her breathing increased. Her rapid heartbeat, presumably because of anaemia secondary to her chronic myelodysplasia, started to falter. At 8.30 pm she passed away. I straightened her body and with rolled towels, supported her chin, dentures intact.

With the family sobbing around me, I rang the on-call doctor. It was an expected death. Could he visit for the certification? When had she last seen her doctor? Over a week ago? Then it is not an expected death. The police would have to be called.

My statement to them was brief, and excluded any mention of medications used to ease her passing. Police would see it as assisted suicide. Of course, I should have called the palliative care team to see if the professor was still available to sanction the use of terminal sedation for perceived existential distress; but it was my mother. I wasn't thinking clearly. I prayed a coroner, a doctor, would see it as an unsupervised act of mercy. My mother was taken away for the autopsy, her dignity and dentures intact.

That was the letter I laboured over. If only I could appeal to a medical authority rather than the perverted lens of the police. The concept of existential distress was, for me, a given. The barrister wasn't so sure and, to my horror, failed to discover any legal precedent or authority. I had thought that my mother's long-held desire to die with her husband and subsequent decision to refuse food or fluid until death ensued, a decision followed more determinedly once her husband had died before her (which had been one of her greatest fears, such was their interdependence) I thought all this would certainly qualify my mother in the same palliative care context in which I had assisted three other people to have inevitable deaths brought forward mercifully under the auspices and legal protection of 'Existential Distress'. When I persisted, however, my legal team drew a blank.

When the recently retired professor was contacted for support, he obfuscated. Suddenly I saw myself at the edge of the abyss. If the medical model couldn't save me, perhaps what I had done *could* be seen as murder. The coroner's report revealed levels of morphine in my mother's blood that may or may not have bought about her death. This level was independent of the timing of doses on the day of her death. A moderate dose as syrup in the morning around nine-thirty and then two more doses given by injection when she was unconscious and dying that evening cannot be differentiated in a total dose. Would I be writing this book, I wondered, in minimum security with the luxury of my own laptop and maybe a small harp?

CHAPTER SEVEN: THE EXPERTS

THE PROSECUTION's briefs to their experts were unlikely to be unbiased, but the murderous twisting of the facts to encourage sinister conclusions was more than misleading. To me, it was criminal. I thought, why let facts ruin a chance to run with evil conjecture? I wanted to avoid hating the person responsible for calling in the dogs, a woman known for her relentless dog-with-a-bone attitude. Certainly, the case of Sue Neill-Fraser had shown a certain intransigence of the Tasmanian Police Force in the face of overwhelming evidence to suggest that they and, more specifically, Linda Mason, the woman who decided to charge and extradite me, the DPP, had got it wrong. I sometimes wondered what malign influence a career in prosecution might have on a person.

In relation to my father, the prosecution maintained that I did not conduct any form of medical examination. My father was semiconscious, clearly dehydrated and lapsing into Cheyne-Stokes breathing before and at my arrival. It was not a time to check blood pressure or call for fresh blood tests.

I don't recall any questioning from the police concerning any medical examinations I may or may not have performed on my father. Further, it was maintained that I refused the assistance of the palliative care team to develop a palliative care plan. Again, with the above symptoms and so close to an uncomplicated death, a palliative care consultation would have not changed his medical management, and would present, to my parents, an unwelcome and unwarranted intrusion.

Further to what I consider a wicked reworking of my father's demise, the police reported that I prevented my mother from giving my father water and his regular medications on the morning of my arrival. I do recall advising just sips of fluid, as he was not conscious enough to swallow effectively and drinking would have led to coughing and distress. Sips of water are enough in the semiconscious to relieve thirst. A family's desire to continue feeding with soft food and fluids into the dying process needs to be tactfully discouraged at times but my father was well past taking food or oral medications.

Completely ignoring the facts that my mother had multiple serious illnesses – including a history of strokes and transient ischaemic attacks – and had not eaten or drunk for a week, the police insisted there was nothing in her medical history to suggest she would have been expected to die. In a one-page timeline of events provided by the police to the forensic pathologist surrounding both my parents' deaths, there is no mention at all that my parents had ceased eating and drinking a week before my father's death. Dark urine and dehydration were noted by his GP a few days before my father died but, again, there was no mention of these important facts in the prosecution briefs. Why complicate a simple case of murder?

I was unable to view the briefing documents provided by the prosecution to the director of a palliative care service in New Zealand whose opinion showed a few omissions of pertinent facts which would have contributed considerably to a skewed judgement of the case. Nor were the police keen to make any distinctions about the timing of the medications given. Subcutaneous drugs were only used in the early evening when Nelda developed Cheyne-Stokes breathing. Somehow, the police believed, and presented as 'evidence', that Nelda Edwards was semiconscious from late morning and was Cheyne-Stokes breathing by mid-afternoon; a squeezing of the facts to make my mother's deterioration in the mid to late afternoon more likely to be seen as a result of medication given in the morning, rather than due to a separate event that occurred in the afternoon. Perhaps a heart attack or stroke had occurred; both highly probable considering her history of malignant hypertension – that is, high blood pressure of unknown cause which is difficult to control despite more than one medication.

My mother moreover could have been cherry-picking her pre-packaged tablets, using the sedatives but not the tablets for blood pressure and high cholesterol and blood-thinning. Who knows?

The prosecution's palliative care specialist listed the medications reported to the police by myself but with no separation in time between oral and subcutaneous doses. Her opinion, 'based on the information provided', was that Nelda Edwards, on the morning of 04/03/2016, was administered sedatives and morphine and died shortly after. Now is that malicious misreporting? Does it come from the police or is it a result of misinterpreting misleading 'evidence', compounding implied murderous intent like a piece of gossip gathering authenticity and greater 'clarity' with each re-telling?

The subcutaneous doses, taken from my deposition before arrest, are misquoted as a total dose given *concurrently*, not *incrementally*, as the same deposition stated; again, implying murderous intent, rather than a graduated response at reasonable doses for a hard-to-miss clinical indicator, Cheyne-Stokes breathing.

The police also stated that I gave my mother these medications for 'existential distress', which I certainly did mention in my police interview three months after her death, and after labouring over my letter to the coroner explaining this concept. But my use of the subcutaneous medication was in response to her obvious clinical condition, and any rationale regarding her state of mind came much later in my grieving process.

When the palliative care specialist states there is no clinical information provided that supports the premise that Nelda Edwards was imminently dying from underlying clinical conditions, then the opinion is as flawed as the clinical information provided. There is no mention of a week's fasting, that is, no food or fluids for a week in an eighty-nine-year-old with multiple medical conditions.

The expert then stated that there was 'evidence' that Nelda Edwards was emotionally distressed and that this was managed using repeated doses of medication to induce unconsciousness and eventually respiratory depression. What a whopping leap of logic is that? What evidence? Hearsay, more likely!

When she said there was no evidence that there was the intent to administer proportionate doses of medication with intent to ameliorate the symptom of emotional distress only, then I disagree with the 'evidence' provided. If my palliative intent was not clear, then I would suggest the lack of 'evidence' provided was at fault.

My mother and father both ceased eating and drinking after hearing of their son Glendon's death a week before their own deaths. Their determination to die was unshakable. Yet the palliative care specialist recommended addressing the 'loss of appetite' by medication to stimulate appetite, and other dietary supportive measures. Is such a comment, so completely off the mark, the result of skewed information provided?

In conclusion, the said specialist opined that although the medications used were common to the practice of palliative medicine, their use in the treatment of emotional distress was not. Again, this was not my intent and is a fault of the 'evidence' provided. Criminal!

Despite some of my mother's specialists omitting items from her extensive medical history, despite my detailed handover to her new GP and careful monitoring of her progress, despite my frequent visiting and reviewing of medical reports, despite taking my mother to appointments with her bowel cancer specialist, the police blithely maintained that I was not up to date with my parents' medical conditions, that I had had no contact with her treating GP and that I was also not up to date with their latest medical tests. So wrong, so insulting, so misleading! Criminal!

The state pathologist deftly declined to get involved in a discussion with the deputy director of public prosecutions regarding the role of medications that I used to ease my father's death as a possible cause of death. He cited my father's advanced prostate cancer, disseminated lymphomatosis complicating a diffuse large B-cell lymphoma, significant atherosclerotic cardiovascular disease and squamous carcinoma of the lung as the causes of death, and that it was not possible to extrapolate, using post-mortem toxicology data, the number of drugs given.

In the post-mortem report on my mother, his precis of events surrounding her death was remarkably free of murderous innuendo. In the description of the examination, he noted signs of dehydration. He carefully excluded any autopsy findings specific to strangulation. Specifically, there were no petechiae or micro-haemorrhages of conjunctiva or periorbital skin, no injuries to the inner, mucosal surfaces of the lips and no soft-tissue injuries to the neck, with both the hyoid bone and thyroid cartilage found intact. Similarly, there were no haemorrhages within the base of the tongue. In accordance with the reported history of fasting, her stomach was found empty.

His opinion as to cause of death was mixed-drug toxicity with significant contributing factors being her atherosclerotic and hypertensive cardiovascular disease, senile cardiac amyloidosis, chronic subdural haematoma, history of multiple falls, post-traumatic seizures and vascular dementia.

His report went on to discuss the level of morphine within the fluid of the eye, a level determined as 0.1 mg/l and then referenced research stating that toxic levels in the eye are reported to be between 0.03–0.8 mg/l, putting my mother in the lower range of toxicity. He then pointed out that the method used to analyse the concentration of morphine in the eye was not fully validated.

When it came to the blood, morphine was found at a concentration of 0.3mg/l. The state pathologist again pointed out that the interpretation of this concentration needed to be done with caution, as there was a significant overlap with morphine concentrations identified in the therapeutic, toxic or fatal cases. Some sources found concentrations between 0.001–0.2mg/l to be therapeutic and levels of 0.3–2.5mg/l to be toxic.

His concluding remarks stated that the complex case presented several possibilities with regard to the cause of death. He cited the advanced natural disease of the heart and blood vessels as sufficient to account for death in many circumstances. A clot found in the heart was a likely complication of her atrial fibrillation, and the possibility of small vessel thrombosis and ischaemia resulting in a fatal cardiac arrhythmia could not be excluded.

He also suggested that another potential cause of death in someone with a history of head-injury-induced seizures was a peri-mortem seizure, and that the risk of such a fit was increased by the recent cessation of preventative medication, as evidenced by the sub-therapeutic level in her blood of the medication used to suppress fitting.

He concluded that it was possible that several or all of these predisposing factors may have contributed to her death by their combined effects. Further, that because of the wide range of values due the varying clearance rates before and after death, the accumulated dose could not be directly related to the cause of death.

This was not the damning report that the prosecution wanted. There were too many wishy-washy areas to argue, many highlighted by the coroner himself. Lots of areas of doubt were clearly not useful to a robust case against me. The prosecution went on to find a forensic physician more inclined to make murderous conclusions.

The information provided to him by the police showed their usual disregard for the truth in setting the stage for murder. In regard to my father's death, the physician was told that at no stage prior to administering drugs did the son of the deceased check his records or speak with any of his specialists. This is an outrageous lie; I had been very involved with the medical progress of both of my parents throughout my adult life as a nurse and then a doctor. I took time out whenever there was another fall to be with them, and supporting and monitoring their progress since. I was more aware than most sons of my father's recent physical decline since the Christmas a few months before his death, of my parents' intransigence regarding institutional care and of the fundamental hopelessness of their situation.

The evening before my father's death, I carefully, respectfully, lovingly washed his body in the bed. The signs of dehydration and Cheyne-Stoking were unmistakable. No expert opinion was needed. The GP was aware of the situation. There was nothing to be done other than ease the way but the prosecution, out of nowhere, insisted, maliciously, that I was not aware of his records or his specialist reports or had conferred with his specialists. This is insulting and a purposeful misrepresentation of the facts. Moreover, they maintained that I did not conduct any form of physical examination when the signs of impending death were clear to me from 'the end of the bed', a medical expression.

The prosecution brief went on to say again that I had refused the assistance of the palliative care team to develop a palliative care plan. Easing death is not rocket science. My experience was attested to by the number of death certificates gathered from my house by the police as evidence. A community nurse, present when I arrived to see my father, offered to contact the palliative care team, which I politely declined. This became a *refusal*, a refusal created to discredit me, another little twisting of the facts to suit a picture of murderous intent.

As already mentioned in the prosecution briefs to other experts, this expert was informed that I prevented my mother from giving Dad any water or his regular oral medications. Malign intent? My father was not fully conscious and not swallowing. Any attempt to do more that wet his lips would have precipitated a coughing fit.

The police went on to maintain that nothing in her medical history suggested that Nelda would have been expected to die. Who made that judgement? Not a medical person – her history held multiple potential causes of imminent death, including autopsy findings of previous strokes, an ongoing intracranial bleed and a clot in one of the chambers of the heart suggesting a heart attack waiting to happen.

Again, the specialist was erroneously informed that I was not up to date with my parents' medical conditions or latest tests and was not in regular contact with the GP, a comment irrelevant to the facts of my father's death, a comment made to denigrate the son who arrived in the nick of time and did nothing more than promised, easing the way to comfortable death.

A senior forensic physician, his presentation of the history from the information provided, showed a complicitous, wilful clouding of the truth in the prosecution's favour. He reported twice that my father had ceased eating, but never mentioned the fact that he had also ceased drinking, a much more relevant detail. Fasting is not immediately lethal but not drinking certainly is, especially in an elderly gent with many other illnesses. The reported fact of his not drinking was validated by blood tests and autopsy findings but not mentioned at all by the physician.

He went on to construct a false history around my father's death, not based on my interview, in which my father was given half-hourly injections and died after three to four doses. My father had intermittent injections through the morning of his death. Two to three became four and the intervals decreased to half-hourly. My father's death was not in question but the physician chose to provide this misleading account of events in the preamble to discussing my mother's death.

In her medical history he made no mention of her chronic myelodysplasia, a terminal condition apparent in the autopsy findings provided to the physician, a condition which was mentioned and made much of by other experts.

In his history of events leading to my mother's death, he again distorts the related details to more easily fit with murderous intent. The four doses of clonazepam given on the morning of her death are increased to several. Is this another example of gossip-worthy 'facts' where the fish gets bigger with each retelling? This is not a fishing story; it is a tale of my innocence or intent to murder. In this blighted report he went on to say, and not in his opinion but as purported fact, that these doses caused her to become unconscious. Where did he get that information?

Although my mother progressed from sleeping and moving her limbs in the morning and during the day to immobility, a previously rapid pulse slowing and then the development of Cheyne-Stokes breathing, no mention is made of even the possibility of an intervening event such as a heart attack or stroke. No mention is made of autopsy findings supportive of this conclusion. No, he finds that Nelda died as a result of high doses of morphine and benzodiazepines, which he notes as confirmed by autopsy.

From his inaccurate retelling of events, he criticises the GP for not exercising closer supervision of my parents' passing, and he found my use of palliative medication prescribed for someone else to be completely inappropriate in my mother's case. Again, lots of room for argument there.

The forensic pathologist garnered by my defence team, a Dr Ringrose, was much more cheerful. Whilst accepting the coroner's suggested cause of death by mixed-drug toxicity as reasonable, he pointed out that this conclusion relied heavily on the veracity of the toxicology results, particularly relating to morphine. Clearly, he found these results debatable.

Moreover, he agreed with the coroner that significant natural disease processes identified at autopsy and involving especially the cardiovascular system would have been 'sufficient to account for death in many circumstances'.

He went on to make particular note of some significant findings, including the old subdural haemorrhage. Examination of the brain showed the bleeds had been ongoing and that there was evidence of an old stroke. Examination of the heart revealed dilation of both atria, chambers of the heart, suggesting chronic hypertension and heart disease and, most tellingly, a blood clot formed before death adherent to the wall of the left atrium. This suggested a heart attack in evolution.

He noted cortical scarring of both kidneys and bilateral nephrosclerosis: kidney damage in this case due to chronic poorly controlled essential hypertension: high blood pressure of unknown cause.

'Marked venous congestion of the liver' pointed to a failing heart and 'narrowing of vessels within the myocardium caused by atherosclerosis and amyloid occupying up to eighty per cent of the blood vessels diameter'. This forms a severe restriction to blood flow that had not been identified prior to autopsy.

Amyloid is a condition of older people where abnormal protein is deposited in various organs, commonly the heart. Perivascular fibrosis of myocardium was also noted: another disease of heart muscle which, when linked with reduced cardiac function as evidenced by the atrial hypertrophy, is associated with progression to heart failure and a poor prognosis meaning, in non-medical language, a rapid and fatal outcome.

He agreed with the state pathologist that a heart attack could not be excluded, as it would not necessarily be identifiable on microscopic examination of the heart muscle.

He also concluded that a seizure associated with the old and ongoing brain injury could potentially result in death and should be considered as a possible cause of death in this case.

Returning to the issues of toxicology, our consultant forensic pathologist went into detail concerning the harvesting of blood from the femoral vein, which may not be representative of the concentrations present at the time of death because of the well-recognised phenomenon of post-mortem redistribution of drugs, particularly morphine, as the post-mortem interval increases.

He went on to suggest the forensic toxicologist should be questioned as to the reliability of the various concentrations and whether or not the blood morphine concentration of 0.3mg/l could have actually been lower and possibly within the therapeutic/non-toxic range. If it were agreed that all the drug concentrations were within the range of accepted therapy, then this would decrease any weight which could be given to the role of drug toxicity in the death of Mrs Edwards. Thank you, Dr Collins.

Our consultant physician with a specialty of pain management, Dr Ringrose, was also pleasantly inclined towards me. He describes thirty years of experience as a physician often caring for patients admitted to hospitals in terminal conditions, and it was his role to care for them as they died. Like me, he attested to caring for hundreds of people in this situation. He emphasised that his role, when it was obvious that people were going to die, was to make sure they did not suffer at all during their dying days. This involved the use of medications similar to those I used. He cautioned that the use of these drugs was mandatory in the conduct of a person dying to ensure they do not suffer unnecessarily. 'Sometimes,' he said, 'one has to use what would be regarded as large doses to achieve this end.'

In listing her concurrent illnesses, the physician spent some time delineating my mother's history of chronic myelodysplasia, a disease including a mixed group of blood disorders where the blood-forming bone marrow is slowly replaced by fibrous or scar-like tissue. It can affect all blood types, red cells, white cells and platelets. Most patients with this condition die as a result of complications related to the decreased blood cells. The prognosis or life expectancy for this disease is extremely poor. Life expectancy when it is diagnosed varies from a few months to a few years. My mother was first diagnosed in 2006.

He also suggested that the initial morphine dose given orally in the morning of 10 mg was not a large dose in the circumstances. He also *disagreed* with the suggestion that the doses of clonazepam were excessive. In his conclusion, he opined that the causes of my mother's death were:

1: Renal failure: Her fluid intake over the week or so prior to death was negligible. She was eighty-eight years old and her kidney function would have rapidly deteriorated with inadequate fluid intake.

2: Myelodysplasia: again, identified as a terminal illness.

3: Cerebrovascular disease: '… significant evidence of widespread cerebral degeneration undoubtably due to arterial problems in a person of advanced age.'

4: Severe hypertension.

5: Atrial fibrillation: rapid, irregular heartbeat.

In his opinion, my mother's death was inevitable. He supported this by referring to her list of serious illnesses compounded by her refusal to take food or fluids for a significant period of time prior to her death and the refusal to take her regular medications. He concluded that although the drug doses used were large, they were appropriate in the circumstances of her death. Thank you, Dr Ringrose.

There is one more report that sheds a strange light on my case, the report of Professor Ashby. Here, I thought, I had an ally, here was the venerable palliative care specialist who once travelled from Hobart to a nursing home in a small town an hour south to hear my patient's plea for merciful medical release. It was a decision he authorised and I had sketched the details of that case in my letter to the coroner. Yet in his declaration he makes no mention of this case and declined comment when I had suggested he may help and he was approached by the team.

The professor was asked by the prosecution whether I had mentioned terminal sedation for existential distress in my dealings with the palliative care team. By way of an answer, the professor described an entirely different case of a home death when I had consulted the team and the professor had been involved. In it, he felt it was an appropriate consultation in a difficult case and that my expertise was consistent with that of a GP with my level of experience in death management. Presumably this had been questioned by the prosecution. The professor was only recently retired. His reasons for not getting into a legal argument on my behalf are his own.

The team representing me put on a persistently positive front. The prosecution had a weak case, they reassured me, a case based on rumour and gossip. Was there a family conspiracy of assisted suicide? None of the three surviving sons was in any financial difficulty, so the inheritance was not really a motive. It is time for some more background detail.

CHAPTER EIGHT: FAMILY CONSPIRACY

My father was an accountant who rose to a government department head and retired on a comfortable superannuation. With the sale of the family beach shack for half a million in 2003 they set up an annuity for my mother, and with the rest they cruised once or twice a year, travelling the world and spending the inheritance, as they say; and with all our encouragement, I should add. My mother loved dressing up and they both enjoyed dancing. It was glorious to see them swimming about together seemingly effortlessly on a dance floor. They always drew comments as a couple and with the demise of dinner dances, the cruise ships provided that lost opportunity for them to kick up their heels.

The cruises became shorter, then stopped altogether after my mother's first major fall. She tumbled down a spiral staircase connecting the house to the garage beneath. Various fractures and a cracked skull with internal bleeding almost led to her death, but holes drilled to release the pressure in her skull saved her life. She struggled hard to regain some childish writing skill and managed to get around the house again with a walking frame.

A woman proud of her knitting, cooking, gardening and housekeeping, she was suddenly deprived of it all. Her gradual decline into old age was suddenly thrown into chaos, but still she maintained a brave face and would quickly straighten her twisted spine using a kitchen bench when visitors arrived. From being a wicked Scrabble player, she was reduced to word-finding puzzles. From one-thousand-piece jigsaws, she could just about manage fifty. We had old family photos reproduced on large wooden jigsaws which she seemed to enjoy.

But still, until only perhaps the last few months, when getting into cabs became too difficult, they had maintained a circuit of places they would go to for lunch. My father budgeted their money well and they did indeed spend the inheritance. After their deaths, when all the debts were cleared, there was little remaining money. They left a sizable house in a better suburb to be divided between four children. It was the division of that money that was at the root of the niece's ill-feeling towards the surviving Edwards family.

Belinda, my brother Glendon's eldest daughter, was bitter. My parents' joint will stipulated that if my elder brother or younger brother were to die before them, the quarter-share each inherited was to go to their wives. But Glendon was divorced; his wife and two daughters had disappeared from family view. Hence, if Glendon died before our parents, his share of the inheritance was to be split between the surviving brothers. This was the share Belinda felt should belong to her and her sister.

The will stipulated similarly for me. If I was to die before my parents, my share also went to the surviving brothers rather than my current partner. My first two relationships, one of seven years, the other of fifteen, were both with well-to-do academics who were grudgingly forgiven by my parents for being male. Glendon would have nothing to do with me, but that was his problem. The last, also fifteen-year relationship, was with an unemployed artist who, after a brief honeymoon period, managed to quickly set himself at odds with my family. Consequently, he was not mentioned in the will. I was unaware of this distinction until after my parents' deaths, but this story concerns the estranged grand-daughter.

There were rumours of Belinda and her sister Elizabeth living in Melbourne as teenagers. Belinda had apparently helped raise her sister's child, now a young man still living in Hobart. He is in intermittent contact with his aunt but unknown to the Edwards family. Papers discovered after my parents died revealed that his care was offered to my parents by the Family Court as a young child at risk. The offer was declined and never spoken of.

No doubt, Belinda did her best to fill in for her sister, but years later this had brewed into bitter resentment. Elizabeth now lives in Queensland raising a seven-year-old daughter alone, while Belinda lives in Brisbane raising her own five-year-old daughter. Their mother also lives somewhere in Queensland. None are currently on speaking terms.

After being informed of her father's death by my brother Leigh, Belinda, who was living in Hobart at the time, was outraged that the will stipulated her father's inheritance was to be divided between the remaining brothers and not go to his children, even though both Belinda and Elizabeth were long unknown to my parents when the will was written.

Her father Glendon had been an intense young man. As a teenager he showed promise as an artist, but also developed some fairly right-wing religious views fuelled by evangelist publications mailed to him from America. Our family were respectable Anglicans, with fairly frequent church attendance until all the children had been confirmed as teenagers. After that, visits to church were for no more than at Christmas, Easter, christenings, marriages and funerals. For Glendon, however, religion became almost a passion; that and his devotion to a high personal standard of physical fitness. A keen sportsman, runner and endurance athlete, he modelled himself on a Clint Eastwood persona: tough and a winner.

Glendon did well at art college and went on to gain a degree in education, beginning a career in art teaching. He married a bright woman with no particular opinions; which was fine, because he held many, often strongly. Sadly, after bearing him two beautiful girls, his wife embarked on a university degree. Perhaps it was psychology. I remember talking to her about *The Female Eunuch* or *The Woman's Room* or some such text. Their relationship fell apart soon after.

After the divorce, Glendon became a full-blown, born-again Christian. Any family interaction involved enthusiastic evangelicalism from him and amused resistance from the rest of us. Glendon gained weekend custody of his children and filled the young girls' heads with religious fervour and the horrors of hell. For him, he and his ex-wife were still married in the eyes of God, so that when their mother dated other men, he denounced her as a slut. When she took out an apprehended violence order to stop him shadowing her in his car, he was fined at least once for breaking the conditions.

His ex-wife then moved to Melbourne, with or without the children. There were stories that the kids hit the streets. Belinda ended up back in Hobart years later. Her father had long gone. After many reprimands, he had been dismissed from the Tasmanian Education Department for the repeated use of physical forms of student management no longer deemed appropriate.

He obtained various overseas teaching positions, often in art but with an emphasis on English, in a series of foreign countries: Japan, Oman and, lastly, Thailand. In Oman, an industrial dispute landed him in jail for three hundred and ninety days where his intransigence prevented all attempts to get him out. Australian and Omani embassies' efforts to repatriate him had failed because of my brother's dogmatic insistence that his grievance against the Sultanate be resolved and compensated before he would agree to leave prison.

When I became aware of the stand-off – a situation kept hidden from us children by our parents out of shame, I think – I pointed out that under international mental health agreements, Glendon could not be held responsible for his own decisions if he was deemed mentally unsound; and any psychiatric assessment performed by the Omanis since his imprisonment would surely have confirmed this.

A document was then found in which a previous psychiatric assessment in Oman had determined that Glendon did, indeed, have psychotic tendencies. Bingo! He was shortly on a flight home to Australia with a psychiatric nurse escort and believing the Australian Government had stepped in to release him while pursuing his case.

For a while he lived quietly with his parents in Hobart, getting teeth replaced and riding a pushbike; but the time in jail with a diet high in white rice had taken a toll. The fat belly he would never have tolerated before prison stayed with him. He had lost some height and stood slightly stooped. His hair had mostly disappeared and what was left was a stringy white. Then he gained a teaching position in a small city in northern Thailand and was gone again.

Glendon wrote long letters to his parents detailing the minutiae of a life dedicated to teaching and his Lord. No real religious fervour seemed to drive him, no epiphany had ever graced his life, but he was content in his faith with no hint of loneliness, rancour or regret.

He was keen to regain his fitness but a long bike ride at night led to a collision with a motorbike, a fractured pelvis and other injuries that began a prolonged time in a Thai hospital. Since then, his recovery had been slow but, like my mother, my brother was nothing if not determined. He continued to take endurance rides on his pushbike until he was found dead on his bed in a rented room, naked in the heat and beginning to smell.

CHAPTER NINE: FAMILY BACKGROUND

It is time to explain myself a little, just to fill in the picture. It is a lot easier talking about others. Of humble roots, our parents were a farmer's daughter and a grocer's son. I had three brothers, all of them athletic; our father was a football umpire. I was the one found in a corner with a book. No-one bothered me about it particularly.

Inspired by a nursing friend of the family and as a ticket out of a rigidly conservative home, I started training as a nurse in Hobart. After a holiday in Sydney, I resigned from Hobart Hospital and returned to complete my training as a registered nurse at Sydney Hospital. Still, I felt something was missing from allopathic medicine. I held reactionary views about doctors in general and the overuse of antibiotics. I was all for vegetarianism, fasting, Bach flower remedies; for herbs and diet as first-line treatments. A year after finishing my training I was working part-time while undertaking a four-year diploma at the British College of Naturopathy and Osteopathy in London.

After returning to Sydney, I quickly became tired of preaching to the converted as a naturopath and wearing myself out as a masseur/osteopath to the stressed and wealthy. I decided to study medicine and join the enemy. Perhaps I could make the world a better place on a personal level.

One of the things that bothered me about doctors while working as a nurse was how out of touch they seemed to be with the dying. Often, they didn't see it coming or denied it when it arrived, as if afraid to admit failure, hesitating over the next step when perhaps that could be to acknowledge death when it arrives and allow it to take its course with honesty, without denial and with the minimum of fuss or interference.

Low light, quiet, family, pain relief – these aren't difficult things to achieve – but we, the medical system, get it so wrong so often that it's more than embarrassing, it's a crime.

I am neither pro nor anti-euthanasia. I am pro death education, freeing the process of dying from the domination of doctors and funeral directors, empowering the bereaved with clear information. I am pro home death, which has fallen from eighty per cent to fifteen per cent in the past fifty years, and not because of a comparable fall in our desired place of death. I do not want an institutionalised, medicalised death.

I also think we have badly mismanaged the care of the aging in our society and was hoping to establish in my career better options of integrated living, of created communities for the aged and infirm, with all these residential options not dependant on economics, or wages or profit margins.

But others are carrying that vision forward. Childcare on site? Who would have thought? Me! I am left to reflect.

I did manage to work with some inspiring people for a few years as a GP registrar in the Sydney Institute of Palliative Medicine, where I gained experience in hospice care and home-death management. Later, when working in Kings Cross, I also had a rewarding time collaborating with a selfless band of nuns who helped the poor and ill, the people who 'fall through the cracks' of the health system and live rough. They were housed and supported by the Brown Nurses and I would be taken on a weekly round of problem solving. I was never a doctor who could sit behind a desk for long.

Now, back to the conspiracy. While our mother was Cheyne-stoking, my elder brother and I were sitting with her, mostly silent, watching her breathing slow and stop, waiting for it to start again long seconds later, only to slow and stop again. There was no groaning or grimacing, no outward signs of distress. The morphine had done its job but still the awful breathing cycle went on and on. I had seen it many times before but my brother had not. He was horrified, sometimes leaning forward as the breathing ceased, only to relax again when it restarted.

There was little I could say to help.

EVIL CONJECTURES

'How long will it go on like this?' he asked. I shrugged my shoulders. 'Hours. Days.'

He moved his chair closer to Nelda's face, took her hand and begged her to let go. He stroked her face, he put his hand over her mouth gently when her breathing ceased, pleading with her to stop; but still the breathing restarted with a gasp. We sat and waited. I turned on lamps in the growing darkness.

Only once did she show any distress. Was it clutching the sheets? It's so long ago now. She settled after a second dose of morphine and midazolam, and a few long hours later her breathing stopped and did not restart. She was dead.

On my return to Phegans Bay, my partner Jamie listened as I recounted the events surrounding her death. The picture of my brother with his hand over our mother's mouth as she was dying took hold in his mind. When I disappeared into prison, this picture in Jamie's head of Robert leaning over his mother with his hand over her mouth became, for him, another possible cause of death.

I left my bank card with car keys for Jamie to collect when I was escorted from Gosford. Once I was in prison, my partner developed a management plan involving a bottle of Cointreau a day and long chats with Agatha, a friend from Tasmania.

Both Jamie and Agatha have had difficult lives that had not left them unscarred. Without delineating the nature of their mental illnesses, they were both prone to exaggeration and overreaction. They got on famously and would talk together for hours.

To be brief, Agatha was at the bail hearing from which I was returned to jail. Belinda was at the same hearing and struck up a conversation with Agatha which led to a boozy dinner in which Agatha revealed the nature of her speculations with Jamie surrounding Robert and his mother's death.

Another friend, a woman who did my accounts in Woy Woy, related when interviewed by police that a pillow over the face had been mentioned by Jamie when she arrived at our Phegans Bay house to collect a painting promised by him. Perhaps the pillow was her unintentional embellishment, but I very much doubt that. When I discovered this detail in her statement in later prosecution disclosures, Jamie insisted that no pillow was mentioned. He, however, lives in a world of constant reinvention and the lady in question, after being interviewed by police and being subpoenaed as a witness, is no longer talking to me.

So here was the rumour the police were so busy working on for the next four years. Belinda made a formal statement to the police in which she made no mention of any foul deeds. A lot was mentioned about the will and how unhelpful Leigh had been regarding her father's death. In her statutory declaration on 11 March 2016, Belinda asserted that when she asked to see my parents' wills, Leigh announced, 'You're not in it, so you don't need to see it.'

Her account of the day she called at my parents' house and my arrival shortly afterwards, the day before my father's death, when he was delirious and bed-bound, was full of inaccuracies, as were a lot of her assumptions about a family with whom she pretended more familiarity than existed. None of it was relevant to the investigation and is not worth dissecting here. I do remember that her presence in the house was upsetting my mother, but I had more pressing matters on my mind and left it to Leigh to usher her out of the house.

Belinda's interview with the police was more telling. She said that all her uncles wanted David and Nelda dead because they wanted her money. Bringing her back to the rumour, the detective reminded Belinda of an earlier interview in which she said Robert held Nelda's nose and mouth until she stopped breathing. Belinda went on. Apparently, Robert's action had taken me by surprise. I had no warning. Robert just did it, it seemed. She discussed the story with her boyfriend at the time, a couple of other friends and her own family before feeling compelled to talk to the police.

Belinda still believes that the rumour she spread is fact because Agatha told her, and also told her that I had told Agatha, not Jamie; or at least, that's how Belinda remembers it.

Sadly, after a long association with the wonderful Tasmanian Harp Society, I faded out. It felt like I was under a black cloud. On bail for murder! I withdrew from workshops, rehearsals and performances, only maintaining contact with one more forthright member who became an invaluable friend. She later helped me spirit away two harps as Jamie slept off a drunken rage. I was leaving the next day, escaping to Sydney and was more worried about the harps than anything else.

Jamie had, in the past, in a fit of pique, cut all the strings on a thirty-six-string harp with kitchen scissors, not including the six metal strings at the bottom – six hundred dollars to replace and hours and hours to restring. I didn't want that to happen again but I couldn't imagine his mood would be good when he woke from drunken slumber the afternoon before I was due to leave him. I rang a harpist friend who drove down, from Hobart to the country town where we lived, in a van equipped to carry harps, as Jamie slept. Only once she had gone was I free to leave the house. I have used the small minstrel harp since to busk in Sydney, just for fun.

Jamie was approached twice by the investigating police for a friendly chat. Once I managed to stop him and shooed the police away. The second time they visited the house to interview Jamie, they may have known I was in court at another fruitless hearing and that Jamie never attended court. Well, he was forbidden after his first performance, when he managed to give a few people a piece of his mind; one to an online reporter who assured us he would not use any of that material, and the other to the junior counsel, a polite young man who looked embarrassed when, a few months later, he asked me to ask Jamie to cease ringing his office and abusing the staff.

When the police arrived at our house for their chat and I was out, Jamie was only too happy to defend me and deflect blame onto my family. It was a dummy spit that led to a police request for audio surveillance: bugging.

Daily abuse from Jamie diminished to weekly as the months of bail stretched into years. How did I get caught up in such a relationship? My two previous relationships ended amicably. This relationship had been volatile from the start. Again, I realised that many people find themselves locked into unhealthy relationships that neither partner is anxious to end. An uneasy truce for the sake of the children, a cold war that can switch to hot in seconds. It is not unknown. I met a couple as patients who argued every point mentioned until the wife laughed and said, 'He's lovely when he's asleep' – adroitly resolving the tension in the room.

I glossed over Jamie's mental illness previously but his flaws or scars or both have left him with high anxiety. Hypervigilant or just jumpy, he is also a chronic insomniac and had almost regular bouts of dry retching soon after waking or when he was especially stressed or just because it was another morning. Certainly, the vomiting had become more regular since bail.

So there I was: locked into a relationship where initially I thought I was helping to stabilise his life and facilitate his painting. How did I get stuck with this smoking cannon? Pull up a chair, make yourself comfortable and I'll explain.

It starts with wanting to help. Some beguiling but feral street kid whom you dress in warm clothing and fix their teeth, perhaps more for the bad breath than their pain, push them to get a driving licence to keep things legal; and, like a rescue dog, they're thankful and you look around and realise there is nothing original in your situation; there are many older men with younger partners who are somehow damaged.

We older men try to moderate the 'behaviours' and drug-taking to our undoing. We support ephemeral ventures bound to fail and we try to fill a deep need for love and security, a safe place, a place of no judgement. But, of course, there is. The judgement of friends: Why doesn't he …? Then the realisation that this is as good as it gets, and to adjust to that: the ongoing compromise between what is acceptable and what is plain nasty, between truth and a created reality with family and friends estranged. I wonder if, without the buffer of progeny to distract and provide purpose, the younger partner assumes the role of an unruly child. Our rescue dogs were marvellous in providing distraction, purpose and, perhaps, some forbearance. The wisdom of taxi drivers: I commented to a cabbie recently that I had no patience and he quickly replied, 'Ah, you have no patience? You have no wife.'

His list of diagnoses put Jamie at high risk of suicide before thirty. Unable to maintain long-term relationships was another attribute of his personality disorder. I got him to a psychiatrist a few times after he arrived in Tasmania and was not coping well. I'm not sure it helped much. When Jamie said no to follow-up, I didn't push it. I got him to counselling a few times, but the counsellors would believe everything he said. When I picked him up from one session, he told me that the lovely counsellor thought he was in an abusive relationship.

Now, nearing fifty, he has hopefully cleared the suicide hurdle, although he will never have much resilience in straitened circumstances, which I have certainly subjected him to. Two months living in a shed, then a year in a barn, before moving into a house for the remaining four years. Two kilometres out of town, the charming old farmhouse, once converted to a gallery, had no internal doors, only a tiny, smoky, slow-combustion fire and a long path through lovely Tasmanian weather to the outside dunny. For four long years. At the end of that time, I found myself trying less to support Jamie and more to harden myself against his regular dummy-spits, the near hysterical temper tantrums and the ongoing abuse of me and my family, both living and dead.

Even now as I write this story from the safety of a studio high above the city, he rang to ask about my health and hear how the book is going. Then the tenor changed. He talked about the two rescue dogs he had to give up after I left; and from there he shifted to blame. Look what I have put him through! When I commiserated, he turned up the loathing. I was a psychopath incapable of compassion … A string of nasty phone texts followed: 'You murdered people, your short stories are dreadful, you fucked both our lives without care, your family are trash, your book won't be published after I talk to the police … I've spoken to them, they're really interested, I'm wishing you a lonely and painful death …'

It's easier now he's not yelling at me, but even at a distance his malevolence is disturbing. I guess it was tough for someone who once confided in a friend that he considered himself a trophy bride. How I laughed when I heard that one! As for the book, he encouraged me to write it, and to write it as it was and to paint him truthfully.

He still believes my mother's death was a family conspiracy that I was drawn into. He is out of what is left of my life now and I can only wish him well. There was a moment, late at night in the middle of those long, cold Tasmanian winters when he realised how much he had 'fucked up' our lives, how he had ruined Robert's and Vivienne's retirement, my younger brother and his wife brought of retirement, how much he had contributed to the mess we were in. But by morning it was gone: my family was evil, I had fucked everything.

Friends helped us through those long years on bail. The emotional toll on both Jamie and I was considerable. After walking the initially one rescue dog, often at a nearby beach, Jamie would suggest a toasted sandwich at the pub. The barmaid, a former nurse manager called Sharon, with a lot of psychiatric experience, could see we were going through hard times. Thankfully, she was fond of Jamie and offered us her friendship. Going through a messy divorce we weathered a few winters at her cosy home and enjoyed her friendship, feeding the slow-combustion fire, stroking her cat, working on her chronic frozen shoulder until it was cured. She bought me a massage table. She took in a big, boofy rescue dog until we could build a dog run.

Sharon tutored me on exit plans and how to manage an abusive relationship. Although she recognised the nature of our relationship, she still had a soft spot for Jamie, who was adept at charming people, mostly until they got wise to his ways or settled into them like Sharon. They both liked talking, and laughed together a lot while I played in her garden. Thank you, Sharon. Couldn't have got through it without you.

The two rescue dogs helped a lot, seeming to arrive just as we were about to kill each other or drive off the road at high speed. Some money turned up from an old superannuation fund. Suggesting friends were helping us out, I replaced the fridge and washing machine in our rented farmhouse and installed a long, deep bath. It all helped but I felt like I was preparing a nest to die in, with a partner regularly screaming at me to hurry up.

After my deadly diagnosis was delivered, I formed an exit plan. I did a death-clean and started writing, waiting for the state border to reopen after COVID had closed it. I was in Sydney a week after the drawbridge was lowered some ten months later. Clothes, books and mementoes of my life made way for court documents.

Jamie, after swearing he would never leave Tasmania, rediscovered his family interstate after I left. When the landlord asked him to leave a few months later he rehoused the rescue dogs, sold the car I had left him and moved interstate to join his family, or so the story goes.

CHAPTER TEN: PRELIMINARY HEARINGS

THE MUCH ANTICIPATED preliminary hearings started on 11 December 2017. They were hard for me to follow. It was not just my poor hearing. I didn't use the headphones provided on request until I noticed others using them later; but still, my head would be in a blur. The proceedings were conducted as if it were a private conversation between friends; uttered *sotto voce* in a foreign language not intended to be followed by the poor victims sitting well away behind huge glass panels. I don't know why they didn't put the morning news on for us, or maybe an old Agatha Christie movie.

It was my brother Leigh who sat each day in court with a pad and pen compiling notes with complimentary doodles that I would later study. I asked him how he managed to get so much down. I used to take minutes was his flat reply.

The first witness for the prosecution was a cleaner for a company dispensing community support to the elderly with gardening, nursing and cleaning services. Amanda was a home care worker responsible for, she stated, minimal cleaning around the house. This did not include any personal care but Amanda had noticed a recent decline in my mother and was aware that 'she had TIA, which is small strokes in the brain', and that she was walking with a walker.'

I remember Amanda. I walked in to my parents' house mid-morning to find my father delirious and dishevelled in bed, a grazed elbow oozing blood through a bandage slipping off, and my mother distraught, trying to get my father up to the toilet so she and the cleaner could help change the bed. Amanda was not helping the chaos and I dismissed her as quickly as I could.

Because Amanda represented a community support service, I did ask if they could access more syringes. They were the only things I could think of that I may have needed more of later. This, sadly, acted as a red flag, an alarm bell, the request generating a flurry of email responses, all reproduced later as 'evidence'.

Evidence of what? Did I dismiss the cleaner too perfunctorily? Was this her revenge, her moment in the spotlight? If I had taken her aside – well, I did – but if I had spent a little longer bringing her up to speed? But my mother was beside herself and my father was mumbling, eyes closed and half-uncovered in a bloodstained bed. Diplomacy was not, to my regret, at the top of my mind.

Amanda made her initial statement on 21 March 2016 but, after thinking some more, she went back to the police on 8 June to again convey her misgivings. She was aware that the other woman present when she arrived on that eventful day was 'an adopted daughter or something'. She noted that Nelda was not speaking in a very kind tone to the young girl and stated that I asked the woman to leave.

It was, in fact, my brother Leigh who explained to Belinda that this was not the time for family chats; perhaps another time. Still, if it was me that asked Belinda to leave it only added to the intrigue created.

After making her statement to the police, Belinda must have indulged in a bit more sinister brooding because an hour later, she returned to the police station to make her third Statutory Declaration. Perhaps it was the microphone? This time she added that, although she was not a nurse, she remembered being horrified because of the stress in the house and being sorry for the young girl turned away. She went on to opine, 'I am terribly distressed by something I believe was not right, that there was a family agreement'.

Well, there you have it. Case solved. Something was not right. Poor adopted daughter turned away at the door. Amanda's day in court arrived.

The barrister defined her role in the organisation of Kincare as a domestic. She had met my mother first as part of her induction in

November 2015 and again eight weeks later, some time in January. She had received no feedback from the carers of my mother within Kincare. The barrister detailed that on 26 February 2016, David rang the service asking for more help. The following day, Kincare became aware of assistance required when the emergency pendant alarm was activated. On 1 March, Kincare management were emailed regarding David's deterioration and a discussion with me was detailed by the barrister. Amanda was not aware of this. She was dismissed from the court.

The next day Miriam Connor, the toxicology laboratory manager, was called. In half an hour of rapid questioning, Miriam conceded the flaws in her reports. She agreed that caution must be used with all her conclusions, that post-mortem redistribution of body fluids can complicate post-mortem analysis, that sampling locations are important and delays in sampling can affect toxicology results, and that drugs do redistribute through the body after death.

The cross-examination continued, concentrating on the morphine concentration, the effect of sampling techniques and the timing of sample-taking. In my mother's case it was over three days, and the longer the period, the greater the redistribution, Miriam agreed. This was followed by a discussion of sample decomposition leading to further inaccuracy.

I remember Miriam. It was all a bit theatrical. The barrister's questioning was delivered rapid-fire while the poor scientist seemed to shrink in her stand, her answers becoming more and more soft and hesitant. She seemed almost in tears before being excused.

The third witness to be called was Judy, a GP I had worked alongside for over a year in 2014. It was a small practice of only a few regular doctors but with a rolling population of locums. By the beach in a classy suburb, the locum job came with an apartment, and some GP's who do locum work in semi-retirement, or as a rotating work option, would spend three months there every year, escaping hotter climes in summer or chasing snow sports in winter.

The original practice had evolved from a solo GP to a group of four. Two or three were locals, including the son of the founding GP, and a locum. When the founding GP retired he left his wife, a registered nurse, to manage reception, while their daughter worked both as a nurse and a receptionist. The clinic was large enough to support two or three practice nurses who could take blood, do minor dressings, administer vaccines, and a whole lot more.

When I left the practice to return to New South Wales, I provided Judy with detailed histories of both my parents on their computer files and orally, with my particular concerns added at that time about my father's continuing to drive and both my parents' increasing dementia and frailty and their refusal to consider any future form of residential care. I thought we got on well, Judy and I, but when alerted to my parents' deaths, she thought the coroner needed to be informed.

In her three-page statement, she chronicled a long history of caring for the devoted couple who always made it clear that if one was to die, that the other would want to die too. She made this point twice in her statement. If one died, the other would want to follow.

Her second point was how unexpected the deaths were. Having not seen my eighty-nine-year-old mother since the previous year, she was surprised to hear of their deaths. She went on to compile a history which showed how out of touch she was with their recent declines, the impact of multiple diseases and increasing dementia in people always careful to present well and with whom she had had no recent contact.

She maintained David was still driving. Three years ago, I wrote to my father's GP at the time, in a different practice, explaining that my father's driving was unsafe and asking that the GP have his licence cancelled. He didn't. One year ago, our dad had a small prang in a carpark, which he denied and promptly forgot. He mentioned Leigh in his argument with the other driver, who sweetly left him to drive home before finding Leigh's number to inform him and swap insurance details. When Leigh informed me of the incident, I insisted he get the car keys off our parents pronto. Poor Leigh! Did *that* lead to some strife?

Judy went on to say that my father was still driving himself and my mother to lunch regularly. Their lunches had been maintained by taxi for some time after father's driving had ceased, but even that stopped altogether some months ago as just too hard. Too hard to get the walker unfolded, the door opened, the chair pulled in.

Unaware of this recent decline, Judy stated that, despite his known history of locally advanced prostate cancer, my ninety-one-year-old father had no life-threatening medical problems and that she had not expected him to die. She had spoken with him on the phone in early January and he had appeared, she said, his normal self. Did she know he had not been eating or drinking for a week prior to death? No.

Nelda, she declared, had only mild dementia despite the added recent deficits following falls and an intracerebral bleed. This she said of a woman who was once a mean Scrabble player, an avid cross-stitcher, a wonderful cook and an active gardener and who had been unsafe in the kitchen for five years or longer with a history of burnt pots, who was unable to prepare food or discern use-by dates, and who was unable to sequence simple tasks. Mild dementia, the doctor said.

Rapid change is a hallmark of caring for the elderly. One day they're chipper; then, suddenly a downturn, and they're gone in a week, or even – and it really does happen quite a lot – die in their sleep. Old people are quite unpredictable in their means of exit. Often sudden, often unexpected, Death arrives without fanfare, like a thief in the night. Nevertheless, Judy was more than surprised by the unexpected deaths – she was extremely surprised.

Given our professional association, Judy was also surprised that I had not thought to contact her with my concerns about my father. I was told by the clinic that Judy had left to take a job with a private nursing home and that a Dr Smith was now caring for my parents. It was clear on the advice given to me by phone by my brother that my father was dying. When confronted by the sight of my father the following day, informing Judy, his ex-GP, of my concerns was not foremost in my mind.

I must admit I was surprised to be so misconstrued by a former colleague. I thought we had a congenial relationship. I had met her flamboyant Spanish pharmacist partner, we had dined with the other doctors of the practice, but now I had become a shady character who had involved the poor locum in a murder investigation. My bail requirements stipulated that I was to have no contact with Doctors Smith or Brown, either the present or another ex-GP.

DOCTOR STEPHEN EDWARDS

I had worked in this clinic for over twelve months. People were genuinely sorry to see me go, both staff and patients. I had a good working relationship with all the nurses. As an ex-nurse myself, I found it was easy to talk the lingo and gain trust and respect. In the short time I worked there I had created many ties with patients who appreciated my honesty and sense of humour. The nursing homes were especially sorry I was leaving but I took Judy around the various institutions I visited, as she was keen to take on this work and this patient load from me on leaving.

But now, I had become the centre of malign gossip, something that grows from suggestion to certainty with each telling. When Judy returned to the clinic for one shift she was informed of the recent deaths, both of which surprised her as unexpected, and after listening to staff concerns, she decided the deaths were suspicious and should be investigated by the coroner.

Under questioning by the barrister for the defence, Judy had to admit she had had no recent contact or knowledge of Mr and Mrs Edwards' health in the months leading to their deaths, and that she was thus not up to date with the relevant information needed to form opinions of any worth.

It was also made clear that, despite the practice writing ongoing scripts for my mother, these were requested and collected by my father and that my mother had not been seen in months, nor had her blood pressure been recorded in the previous six months, despite a generally high reading when checked and her receiving more than one medication for hypertension. In half an hour, after her grasp of the elderly couple was called into question, Judy was excused.

A certain nurse in the same practice, we'll call her Jackie, was also deeply suspicious about the deaths and keen to make a three-page statement to the police.

Having joined the clinic after I had left, she recalled hearing about a previous doctor, Dr Stephen Edwards. She stated this was just rumour from other staff that he was a strange character. Not flamboyant, colourful, amusing, lively, well-dressed or popular with the patients. Perhaps he was a homosexual? Oh, no! A strange character, no less. What exactly did you mean by that, Jackie?

Swept away with importance, Jackie went on to say she believed I had rung the practice on 29 February 2016 and that she had answered the phone. Keen to be seen as a reliable witness, she admitted she was not sure if I had rung from a landline, phone box or mobile. She then related how, the next day, I had rung from the pharmacy next door, where I was collecting the medications that I had asked the GP, Dr Smith, to organise. GPs generally don't have the authority to write scripts in more than one state. I had rung to organise to see the GP, and Jackie explained that he was with someone but would pass my message on to him if I could wait.

After I saw the locum and explained the state my father was in, he asked Jackie to help me select some needles and syringes I would need. I explained to the nurse that I was palliating my father and left shortly afterwards.

Jackie went on to add that she had seen both my parents in the waiting room twice in the week prior to their deaths; which is surprising, since my father had attended the surgery alone only once in that week. Jackie further recalled that my father was complaining of pain from, she thought, bowel cancer, and in her opinion, he looked OK and was just complaining of pain. He didn't look particularly sick to her.

Jackie wrote in her statement to the police that she felt that both Johnny (the locum) and her had been set up. She felt I hadn't told the truth as to why I wanted the needles and syringes. She added that I could have bought my own needles and syringes. She finished her statement by saying she had since spoken to the GP and she understood he felt the same way.

Well, that settles it then. Thanks, Jackie. Sadly, the preliminary hearings were cut short and Jackie's medical assessment and other opinions would never be publicly explored.

The next witness to be called by the defence was Dr David Dunbabbin, a geriatrician who became involved in my mother's care following her admission to hospital in 2013. She had fallen down an internal staircase, sustaining not only an arm broken in two places but an intracranial bleed requiring burr holes. The questioning over the next hour seemed to be in order to confirm the number and severity of the illnesses plaguing her.

On the following day a video link was established with the locum Dr Smith, who was now working interstate. The questioning quickly established that the locum had a very imperfect recall of my mother's complex medical history; but without his computer records, this was hardly surprising.

It was revealed that the GP had first met my mother on 28 January 2016 during a joint visit with my father that lasted under fifteen minutes. My father would have done all the talking. I'm sure Mrs Edwards would have 'presented well', as we say in the business. My mother would not have gone to the letterbox, much less visit a doctor, without being well dressed with a touch of make-up and a dab of scent. He did not see her again until called to certify my father's death, at which time he naturally did not examine my mother.

The only other contact my mother had with the GP was a phone conversation in which she expressed distress over the death of her son and wanted an injection, without directly stating a wish for euthanasia as such. The locum was aware that my father had fallen out of bed shortly before my arrival and was then virtually bed-bound but still refusing to go to hospital. The locum was asked if he had treated my mother for many issues. He could only recall writing continuing scripts for multiple medications for my mother on requests from my father, but he had left no record of blood pressure readings or any other issues discussed regarding my mother.

Further preliminary hearings were stopped without warning the following day when the deputy public prosecutor informed the court that further information from the Tasmanian Police impacted on Dr Edwards and may delay the trial, and that any further appropriate charges would affect the trial dates. Linda Mason claimed that evidence obtained by police impacted on the nature of the charges and may involve laying further charges on other people whom the Tasmanian Police had been investigating for some time.

The court was adjourned for six weeks. A month later, my eldest brother, Robert, was charged with common assault. It seems it was the best the police could come up with in response to the rumour of asphyxiation;

and a way, with an added police car pursuit and arrest, to intimidate recently retired Robert. Robert was charged on 22 January 2018 and phone-tapping and home audio surveillance was initiated for twenty-four months. With no evidence and no autopsy findings to support it, the charge of common assault was eventually changed to conspiracy, but more on that in the next chapter.

CHAPTER ELEVEN: THE PROSECUTION LINE-UP

THE PRESS were allowed to be present during all the court proceedings but were forbidden to comment on the substance of those discussions until the case was clearer, for fear of influencing future jurors.

The list of witnesses for the prosecution was long, at one stage nearing fifty. The number of statements was daunting but mostly they seemed inconsequential, of little relevance or importance; but opinions regarding the case were gathered nonetheless. Here is a sample.

A hairdresser thought, from what my mother had confided from the chair, that it was a case of suicide, although she did go on to describe my mother as a very fragile lady.

A restaurant manager noted my father's recent decline, describing him as frail. In a private conversation, he later revealed to me that my mother had rung him the day after my father died. Thinking back, it must have been when she had sent the sons and daughters-in-law out to lunch. She rang him to thank him for all the years he had made a fuss over them both. They ate there once a week. He had napkin rings engraved with their names. After my mother had rung, demented but polite until the end, he heard of her death the following day but said nothing until visited by the police who questioned him along with many others in the catering business.

The manager of a yacht club where they ate said my parents appeared in good health and he was surprised to hear of their deaths. The manager of The Doctor Syntax, a hotel restaurant, had a first-names friendship with them and said they seemed well, although David had mentioned that if Nelda died, he didn't want to be without her for very long.

Another restaurant owner commented that David was looking frail and needed help getting up from the table. He too was surprised by Nelda's death but then said she had become slower to respond and more hesitant in her movements.

Virginia, a waitress noted my mother's dementia, relating how she had talked about her children as if they were still little. She thought Mr Edwards looked sick: yellow and cold on a warm day. She recalled my father saying, 'If only we could take a pill!'

One manager recalled that my father had had trouble remembering his PIN but was still surprised to hear of their deaths. A taxi driver had lately found my father more vague and not his normal self but said his wife looked well.

I'm not sure what the prosecution wanted to achieve with this line-up. My parents' opinions regarding euthanasia were well known. Sadly, they didn't repeat my response to this often- repeated refrain, which was that I wouldn't help with that but that I would be there to ease the way when their times came. This was usually said with sarcastic jokes added about the car in the basement. Dead funny? After their licences were finally given up, the car was quickly sold.

My parents made their position on euthanasia clear to anyone and everyone who would listen. They knew all the terminology without any prompting from me. Here is an application that My father completed for my mother to appoint him as her guardian in 2003:

The document was clear. '… in the event that I become unable by reason of a disability to make reasonable judgements … I require my guardian to observe the following conditions …'

He wrote:
i. To confer with Dr Stephen John Edwards on any matters/decisions concerning my health and welfare.
ii. I do not wish to be placed in a supported residence.
iii. I do not wish to have any lifesaving or prolonging medical intervention in the event my health deteriorates to the point of becoming irreversibly incontinent and or mobile [I'm sure he meant *immobile*. He was affected by dementia at the time.]

iv. I do not wish any steps to be taken to prolong my life or any unnecessary palliative care measures to be taken, including any operations of any kind. I believe in euthanasia.

v. I request all life systems to be withdrawn if my son, Dr SJ Edwards, concludes any illness is terminal and my life be terminated. This request also applies to any medical condition that leaves me totally incapacitated, physically or mentally.

vi. I have legally bequeathed my body to the University of Tasmania – I am a registered organ donor.

vii. I wish my ashes to be scattered …

He was certainly trying to cover every option there, but the document also suggests a little dementia was already creeping in, even from that long ago. 'Our son, the doctor'. They were so proud but, over and over, I told them not to involve me in their plans.

They were quite fond, I suspect, of shocking polite company with their radical views on euthanasia and body donation. Even a hairdresser got the story. But did the prosecution believe that a compilation of negative opinions amounted to evidence, and that a procession of witnesses would sway a jury to believe I was complicit? It would seem so.

There was one witness for the prosecution, an astoundingly uninformed gentleman called Billie, the undertaker's assistant, who deserves some description. After three years of refining the craft of transferring bodies from bed to trolley to van, he was very keen to offer his opinion and insights into the case.

In the process of removing my father's body, Billie had managed to jam his finger in the trolley mechanism, leading to a minor graze. He was impressed that Nelda noticed the cut from a few metres away and, mentioning that she had been a nurse, directed her son Leigh to fetch a Band-Aid, which he applied for Billie.

Billie carefully noted that the deceased was lying in bed with the covers up to his chest. He was wearing full-length pyjamas and no jewellery. He didn't observe any blood or signs of trauma or any puncture marks. I'm very glad I didn't see him check the body.

Billie went on to observe that although my mother was steadying herself with the furniture, she was moving well and was coherent, making sense and appearing to comprehend what was going on. She remembered Billie from a recent funeral, demonstrating that her memory seemed good and she had no obvious signs of dementia. He went on. She wasn't coughing, wheezing and didn't appear unwell or injured in any way. He wouldn't have guessed she was eighty-eight and thought she looked only eighty.

Billie's first impression on entering the house was that the death was not unexpected and there was no overwhelming grief. I don't think we are an over-restrained family but, as far as I was concerned, a stranger was in the house to remove my father's body. Did he expect extravagant displays of grief? After leaving the house, he recalled hearing Nelda's really distressed howling and crying. More to his liking, perhaps? When he left in the van, he remembered how they commented that we appeared like a family that wasn't ready to say goodbye to their loved one.

How is this relevant? Why was his declaration included as evidence? An undertaker's assistant declares my mother has no obvious signs of dementia. Well, thank you for that insight, Billie. To make sure his point was clear, however, in the last paragraph of his three-page document he stated that he was surprised at the sudden death of Nelda as she didn't appear unwell or have the appearance of a person who was close to death. Dealing with up to five hundred deaths a year, Billie couldn't recall a single person dying of a broken heart within days of their partner passing. Very unusual, he declared. Right, then!

CHAPTER TWELVE: THE MEDICAL INSURER

THE ISSUE of medical insurance came about because I didn't talk to them prior to my arrest. I didn't ring them and say, look what I've done! I was like a rabbit in the headlights, frozen, working hard to catch up with all the nursing home patients who didn't wait for my return to have incidents that needed attention.

I knew I had 'fucked up' as my partner kept reminding me. I wondered desperately if I could talk my way out of it in some coroner's court or before a bench of benevolent doctors. I believed I was innocent. Surely I could convince others? When I was thrown into jail after announcing I was off to France, my eldest brother engaged a reputable barrister. When I contacted my medical insurance company from inside jail, I was told, after the barrister was reviewed and approved, that the insurer, AVANT, would cover my legal expenses.

My team presented AVANT with the bills to date but no money was forthcoming. I held to the idea that AVANT would soon or eventually come to the rescue and refund the money my brothers and I were spending on legal fees. While still in jail, the sale of my parents' house afforded a fighting fund of $150,000 to the defence team of two, the silk and a junior solicitor, who was doing a lot of the routine paperwork. After pressuring, AVANT denied any previous agreement and refused to cover me. And, of course, the fighting fund, originally calculated as more than sufficient, was, with the prolongation of the case, getting close to zero.

It was a gamble but we – the team and I – decided it was worth pursuing the matter of insurance in court. As the projected length of the trial grew, so did the number of staff that would be needed to properly manage the documents during the trial and other activities. The expected expenses were enormous, the barrister's daily fee for appearing in my behalf was staggering.

I found a friend willing to put up the expected $50,000 to take the insurers to court in the hope of recouping our expenses. As a separate action, we were advised it would cost up to this amount. Unfortunately, it was not a separate action at all and culminated in a kangaroo court where I and the solicitor were required to attend a friendly chat over details of my mother's death.

It was after a court hearing that was little more than an expensive exchange of documents.

Summoned to an informal meeting, the solicitor and I arrived at an office block to find ourselves in an enormous but empty conference room with expansive views across the harbour and audio-visuals linked to head office in Melbourne. A female flunky conducted the interview while a male, mostly silent, sat at the back of the room after introducing himself in a mumble and trying out a few reassuring phrases before the interview proper began. We only want to help. Toilets on the left.

Again, I talked through that fateful day. The invisible and, no doubt, hung jury delivered their judgement a few days later. No. We took them to court again. It became clear that they could throw more and more money into the ring and could prolong the case well past our financial capacity. It was like a game of poker where the money you wager is matched and upped again. We withdrew when the $50.000 was nearly exhausted and, fortunately, AVANT allowed the case to close without incurring further expenses.

Thank the heavens, I had an unexpected superannuation payment after the case was dropped and was able to recompense my friend most of her $50.000. My brothers will have to wait until the dividends of the book are forthcoming before they can recoup any of the inheritance of which I robbed them.

CHAPTER THIRTEEN: THE INVESTIGATION

With such unconvincing witnesses, the police were keen to track down my letter to the coroner. I mentioned to both my partner Jamie and my brother, while still in prison, that this was my defence fall-back. Aha, they must have thought, a written confession. They later thought to check my hard drive, as I've said, but not before dispatching two detectives to New South Wales to interview my friends there, trying to find a copy of this letter which, I mentioned, even while knowing that prison calls were monitored, I had left with someone for safe-keeping. What the police discovered instead were more than a few friends who were more than happy to discredit my 'loopy' partner and no sign of a letter.

One good friend who took Jamie in for a week after I was arrested – Jamie was such a mess – stated delicately that Jamie liked a drink. Another friend suggested that although Jamie was a 'bit of a character, he was also a mess'. When asked if Jamie said anything unusual in the time between my mother's death and my arrest, he answered, 'He was unusual all the time.'

A close artist friend described Jamie as 'very, very' unusual. 'Jamie is very about Jamie, and we love him dearly. But you? Jamie is centred on Jamie, so he will tell you about him and his family and all the rest of it; so every now and then I got a word in. I do love you, Jamie. Sometimes.'

The police interviewed Margaret, a recently retired director of nursing who had become a close personal friend after we had worked alongside each other for five years. She stated that Jamie had told her that my brother Robert had put a pillow over my mother's face. When asked what was Jamie's state of mind, she replied, 'Oh, he was agitated, really agitated. But Jamie can be like that anyway. Life isn't smooth for Jamie.' She went on to say, 'I just don't believe that Stephen would do anything like that, especially not his mother, because he was so fond of her.' Certainly, I was fond of both my parents.

When asked how she would describe my knowledge in the area of palliative care, Margaret replied that it was an area that I was interested in and, in her experience, I did it very well. She was never concerned that my management was inappropriate.

Regarding Jamie and the rumour, Margaret asked, 'How would Jamie know, really? Was that Jamie being dramatic? Very likely.'

Audio surveillance commenced after the police had their chat with Jamie when I was absent. Jamie had spat the dummy, as they say, regarding my family and a lot else besides. He told me the dog wouldn't get out of the police car, hence his extended rant. He refused to make a statement, however, declaring himself an alcoholic with PTSD, but enough had been said to prompt an application to bug our and my brother Robert's houses.

Years of bugging meant that some poor person had to listen to it all to extract a few nasty arguments in which some family dirty washing was aired, which I would rather not have been obliged to read. But no identifiable confessions or indications of complicity were found to suggest a family plot to knock off mother, or mother *and* father. I had even heard of suggestions on the net that I was also involved in the death of my brother in Thailand, but I can't say the police were involved with that speculation.

CHAPTER FOURTEEN: THE COURT HEARINGS

THIRTY-TWO separate hearings were held over the next four years.

At the first hearing, on 14 February 2018, Linda Mason informed the court that the police were continuing their investigations. The judge suggested a further directions hearing in four weeks. Mason suggested six, and a date six weeks hence was chosen.

26 March 2018: No record of this hearing. Perhaps it was cancelled.

27 June 2018: At a further directions hearing regarding Robert, Mason promised to produce new material by the end of the following week. The assault was not linked to my murder charge. His case was adjourned until 21 August 2018.

At a directions hearing for Robert on 23 July 2018, there was some discussion of my mother's autopsy report, yet to be received by the defence. A final decision on the charges to be faced by Robert was expected soon. The case was adjourned until 8 August.

On that day, the barrister appearing for Robert noted he had received a brief from the Crown consisting mainly of a statement by Jamie – my dear, crazy partner – but to confuse matters, he said that it included nothing derogatory to Robert. A decision on the final charges had not been finalised. Mason instructed that a decision would not be made until 21 August because the prosecution, then two years and two months after my arrest, were *still* reviewing the case. Cryptic references were made from the Crown to the judge.

Robert's barrister made the point that each appearance cost Robert a lot of money, and perhaps the Crown could articulate their position. They could not. The case was adjourned until 21 August.

The date of the next appearance was 3 September 2018. We were informed that an indictment had been filed. Hundreds of hours of 'listening' needed to be transcribed. My barrister declared the defence was ready for trial. The Crown expected the trial to last at least four weeks.

With no evidence from the autopsy of any sinister trauma, Robert's charge of assault, based only on hearsay from people of doubtful integrity, was changed to conspiracy. Conspiracy to conceal evidence from the Crown. Robert's barrister said he would need fuller disclosure to review the 'evidence' before the preliminary hearing could proceed.

At a directions hearing held on 8 October 2018, Robert's barrister informed the court that he was only very recently in receipt of volumes of 'evidence' provided by the prosecution and was still reviewing that material. This material was also released to me. Forbiddingly huge files of irrelevant witness statements full of nasty innuendo with hours of transcribed audio surveillance of two couples with the occasional outbursts of relationships under stress; conveniently highlighted but of no substance relevant to any evil family plotting. My twenty-two short stories alone consisted of dense prose which had been combed for any euthanistic evangelism without success. There is none. But, still, twenty-two stories concerned only with death? Sadly, from all the people forced to read them at speed, a concentrated dose of things that go wrong, I received not one review, neither good nor bad.

The barrister was, not surprisingly, yet to form an opinion. He did, however, favour the separation of the cases. Mason saw no difficulty with assembling witnesses for 19 March 2019 for a trial she now expected to take four to five weeks, although the separation of charges could change that timing.

The next hearing was set for a date two weeks hence. It was merely a side issue that, after repeated requests for evidence, Robert's barrister was given just two weeks to consider some fifteen hundred pages of transcripts and statements.

On 6 November 2018, Mason informed the court that it would take another four weeks at least to prepare further transcripts of the listening devices, telephones and mobiles, now expected to exceed six volumes. More dirty laundry? Great!

My barrister applied to sever the cases so that the murder trial could commence. He also requested complete disclosure prior to trial and that this was required hopefully by 3 December 2018. 'Required hopefully?' Maybe a transcription error.

Robert's barrister suggested a separate trial, once the cases were severed, which would take two to three days with possibly two witnesses. The murder trial, it was further suggested, should precede the conspiracy case.

At a directions hearing on 4 February 2019, the judge wanted, 'Just to check where we are.' Robert's barrister again asked for severance. On the balance, he argued, the cases being joined was prejudicial to his client. The application for severance, it was decided, could be heard within eight weeks.

There was some to and fro about my finances and applying for legal aid after an action against my medical insurers failed, but more of that later. The case was adjourned for another two months. The next hearing was to be 1 April 2019 but was then delayed a further two weeks.

On 15 April 2019, much discussion was made around the allocation of court dates. Linda Mason suggested preliminary witnesses could be heard around Easter and that the legal argument, before the trial proper, was expected to last three days and would be heard *'this year'*. Jolly good, no rush! This time the criminal court case was estimated by Linda Mason to take nine weeks. Severance was again mentioned. Somehow my representation was required in this but, I must admit, a lot of the court proceedings at this point – often inaudible with many whispered asides between the parties and the judge – a lot of what was said went completely over my head. And in the end, what did it matter? The case was adjourned.

At a directions hearing on 5 August 2019, Linda Mason then felt the trial could be held in March 2020. The civil case was yet to be determined. Severance of the civil case from the criminal case was expected in November–December. There was some discussion around holidays of both prosecution and defence team members. Then, in further discussion, it was decided that the severance hearing could be brought forward to 3 October. Wow! Won't the kiddies be pleased? Case adjourned.

On 2 December 2019, the new barrister from legal aid said she was in recent receipt of eleven volumes of Crown papers. She met with the barrister representing my brother three days previously but had been unable to complete a review of the court documents; which had not, in fact, been released and delivered to her until the day before today's hearing. That was yesterday. There wasn't any real purpose for the hearing today, a hearing purposefully stymied by the prosecution at great expense to myself. The judge called for a prompt decision. Of what, I'm unsure. My future? Bail was to continue.

On 4 December, the prosecution delivered, with no fanfare, as if reciting a shopping list, a summary of their case against me: I had admitted to administering a cocktail of drugs to my mother. I think a *cocktail* of only two medications a bit melodramatic, but perhaps that explained the off-hand delivery. I administered the cocktail knowing it could lead to death? Well, no. The tablets and syrup given in the morning were for sleep and pain relief. The two standard medications given subcutaneously when my mother was dying that evening were given in response to her dying, not to cause it, a fundamental point persistently ignored by the prosecution.

The letter to the coroner was presented by the prosecution as a personal admission of terminal sedation as a motive. My use of the medications was described as reckless. By witnessing me giving some of the medication and not discussing this with police when our mother's body was removed, the Crown alleged collusion to pervert the course of justice, adding something about the consciousness of guilt and conspiracy.

My barrister asked, what is your evidence? The judge said an agreement was questionable. An agreement must have been in existence.

The Crown alleged that I had made misleading statements to avoid prosecution. Did I lie to direct questioning? No.

My brother's barrister asked for a suppression order for media. Reporting of procedural detail was allowed and coverage of the preliminary, presumably legal, argument was promised.

The prosecution went on to mention a card from my brother Robert found by the police in my messy home office in Phegans Bay, near Woy Woy. It was a condolence card, entirely innocent of any implied intent, but the police thought it somehow confirmed an awareness that I contributed to our mother's death. Was this the strength of their 'evidence'?

The drugs were administered to relieve existential distress, the prosecution stated; but, although I did call up the concept after my mother's death in the letter to the coroner, it was never presented as my motive at the time. Although they concede this to be a legitimate palliative care concern, they maintain that palliative care could potentially be subtly different to terminal sedation.

Before my arrest I had confided in a nursing colleague over a cup of tea that I was worried about the upcoming autopsy because, and I quote from her statement to the police, that, 'I shouldn't have used such big doses'. Let me say in retrospect that they were generous doses, but my mother was dying and the dosages didn't really matter. They were not outside the normal ball park of dosages, as our palliative care specialist pointed out. Still, this quote was introduced as damning evidence.

Of all the hours of listening from the years of audio surveillance of two houses and two phones, all that was collected and typed up contained nothing more than some family dirty washing. Stressed couples having heated arguments in which not the nicest things were said about other family members was difficult reading, but had no direct impact on the case. Only one dummy-spit, an argument between Robert and his wife Vivienne, had any relevance that could be read as tenuously useful to the case. But Robert's barrister suggested the conversation between the accused and his wife was inadmissible and, since the deputy public prosecutor agreed, there was no need to explore heated remarks any further.

The judge pointed out that if the criminal case verdict was returned as 'not guilty', then the Crown could argue that the civil case may then proceed.

The defence, in reference to the charge of conspiracy, suggested that the Crown needed to define an agreement. They submitted that, of the substantive charge, the Crown had failed to produce any evidence of an agreement.

There followed some discussion on why the cases should be separated. Evidence that could prejudice a jury was cited. My barrister went on to suggest that further information potentially prejudicial to a jury included interviews pursuing a financial motive, details of Glendon's death, medication and listening devices.

The barrister for my brother talked about principles of conspiracy, referring to a previous case; but in this instance the point of the case and the discussion were lost on both myself and my rapid-minute-taking brother.

Somehow, it was agreed that Belinda's evidence was inadmissible. Further, that Robert's wife Vivienne was compellable and competent to give evidence, but *not* against her husband. All those pages and pages of transcribing! All Belinda's murderous rumour-mongering. All suddenly inadmissible. Just like that, over without discussion in less than a minute. I wonder how Linda felt at that moment.

My collection of short stories concerning death, all of them actual cases I wanted to publish as you-need-to-know-this stories, had been found on my hard drive and construed as evidence – of what, a familiarity with death? The prosecution suggested it demonstrated a previous tendency for similar activity, referring to my three cases of medically (and, I thought, legally) sanctioned terminal sedation. Mason talked about an understanding, a state of knowledge, and of best practice, but in the end, she agreed not to use my short stories as evidence of anything.

These stories were actually very important to me. I once worked with a GP who was also an author and great raconteur, Dr Ray Seidler. He said to me, you will hear a lot of stories working in Kings Cross. Write them down! The practice of writing became, for me, a way of recording all the admirable or interesting people I met and the odd events that occur and difficult deaths I witnessed. The stories concerning death I gathered into a collection I was intending to publish, a collection that the prosecution seized upon.

As I have said, I am not an advocate of euthanasia, but I do think we manage old age and death badly in Australia and that education around death and its de-medicalisation would help reduce the gap between those who want to die at home and those who manage it. But that is another story.

Maybe my collection of stories, twenty-two so far and all involving incidents from my working life which happened to include death, maybe these stories were a sign of something more sinister? An unhealthy obsession, perhaps? Using the same reasoning, how would Linda Mason account for those dedicated people working at the coalface of death? Palliative care is a specialty that still struggles for recognition, an area always understaffed by the most wonderfully caring people. Hospice workers deal with death every working day. They are angels. How do they do it? Why do they do it?

They say in medicine that you don't find a speciality; it finds you. My experiences as a nurse showed me how badly death was managed in hospitals and nursing homes. I wanted to change that and was drawn to palliative care during my undergraduate training. I met inspiring people in the field. A GP on the Central Coast had built a network of cancer centres where food, massage and information were dispensed. Dedicated palliative care beds were allocated in the regional hospital. Nurses, registrars (doctors in specialty training) and the elderly GP oversaw a huge catchment area (not my term) with home management a primary role of the service. The local centres provided support and a sense of community for those suddenly alone with a diagnosis of death at the door. But, back to the story.

There was a lot more discussion regarding overlay or overlap and admissibility versus severance, all of which was way over my head. The judge ruled that autopsy findings and any evidence relating the cause of death to myself was not relevant to the civil case and may be prejudicial.

There followed a strange summing-up of my legal options. It seemed that, apart from murder, I could be accused of using terminal sedation for either an unlawful killing or a legitimate use of palliative care.

On 5 December, further discussion was made about what was admissible as evidence and what was not. A page of carefully written notes in pencil revealed little more to me than, 'There is no evidence of an agreement between Robert and Stephen Edwards.'

After reference to previous cases, the inflammatory material from the intercepts of Robert and Vivienne Edwards was to be removed.

The judge made a decision regarding the underlying issues of admissibility as needing review. That means that he decided the issue needed a decision. He promised a decision by 19 December. After discussion of possible trial dates, my barrister this time suggested a new trial length estimate of between seven to eight weeks. What fun they were planning! The daily headlines, the gritty black and white photos of determined faces in flowing black gowns.

The media suppression was to continue until the first day of the trial. Case adjourned.

On 2 June 2019, my liver cancer was revealed with a prognosis then of six to thirteen months.

A draft trial plan of four weeks was reported as on track, expecting to last from 16 March 2020 until 9 April.

The phone-intercept admissibility had still not been decided but a decision was promised by trial commencement, and possibly beforehand. The judge declared no need for further listing, with the trial date set for 10am on 16 March.

On 2 April the nolle prosequi was announced: case dismissed on medical grounds. To destroy any impression of the prosecution withdrawing before defeat, a media release from the Crown informed us that they, the police, were not pursuing the charges because of the public interest issue, not because there wasn't sufficient evidence to prosecute. Specifically:

THE STATE OF TASMANIA v STEPHEN JOHN EDWARDS and ROBERT DAVID EDWARDS

The Director of Public Prosecutions has decided not to proceed further on the indictment and asks that both the accused be discharged.

In respect of both accused, this decision was not made on the basis of the available evidence but on public interest grounds. This matter was due to commence for trial on 16 March 2020. Of course, no trial now would be in any event commenced for many months.

In February 2020 counsel for Mr Stephen Edwards informed the Office of the Director of Public Prosecutions that Stephen Edwards was gravely ill. A report from his treating specialist was provided to Crown counsel which confirmed this. Further information was obtained from his treating specialist and general practitioner and supplied to counsel from the ODPP that confirmed in essence, that he would have difficulty in giving instructions to his counsel, he would not be able to do justice as a witness and the trial itself may cause the accused's condition to deteriorate.

As a result, the Director engaged an eminent specialist from St Vincent's Hospital in Sydney. He examined Mr Edwards' medical records and came to the same conclusions as Mr Edwards' treating specialist.

The Director has as a result concluded that despite the serious charges, it is now not in the public interest to proceed with the indictment. The Director has concluded, given the nature of the illness, the prognosis, the fact that he is unlikely to be fit to stand trial in the future, it would be oppressive to continue with the both charges of murder and conspiracy to pervert the course of justice. The Director is satisfied that Mr Stephen Edwards does not pose a risk for future offending.

In respect of Robert Edwards, the Director has also concluded it would not be in the public interest to proceed with the charge of conspiracy to pervert the course of justice (count 2) on the indictment. He has concluded that as there will not be a trial involving the alleged principal offender, and as the Crown case was that Mr Robert Edwards was not the instigator of the conspiracy, a significant time has now passed since the alleged offence, any trial would be extremely lengthy and given the subsequent delay in court trials, it would be unfair to proceed against Mr Robert Edwards.

D G Coates SC

DIRECTOR OF PUBLIC PROSECUTIONS

26 March 2020: They protest too much? That was *it*, folks. Case dropped, and not because we couldn't get him.

I was also advised that the police would say that the four years on bail was because *my* legal team had delayed the prosecution. They would also maintain that the charges were validly laid and, in those circumstances, there would be nothing to compensate. Loss of career, relationship, house and health was entirely my doing, not theirs.

The Tasmanian Police Force is the only state police force in Australia that is above investigation for wrongful arrest. A police force with no external constraints and above the law. How is that? I wonder. Why is that?

EPILOGUE

THREE LAWYERS, one an activist and a regular local newspaper contributor, all of them advised me to stay quiet or incur the wrath of the Tasmanian Police, who could make my remaining time alive as miserable as they have done for others quoted to me who – in similar circumstances, once cleared – dared to question a bungled investigation.

I was specifically warned that the Tasmanian Police would likely smear my reputation – or worse – in response to any proposed publication. I went away. I curled up under a rock, as they say, nursing my cancer.

How close to death did I need to be to be beyond harassment? I wondered. Now, some of my tumours are shrinking, some are quiescent while others appear. A new whiz-bang intravenous therapy was started. Every three weeks I sat back for a few hours to receive a toxic infusion, two drugs for the price of one with a list of possible side effects long enough to cause more. I could list nine – ten, if you include rancour. Would I lose my hair as well as my reputation? Will I have time to finish this book?

The one day I woke up seeing rainbows and feeling a bit wobbly. Not good, I thought, and managed to get a cab to the local hospital where, once I had been clerked into Casualty, I promptly fell unconscious to the floor and had a fit, all due to high blood pressure secondary to treatment.

It was only two days later that a fractured arm was discovered. I managed to get discharged a few days later and the offending treatment was suspended.

All was quiescent for a while but when my legs began to swell again I knew the cancer was growing back into my Inferior Vena Cava, the main vein draining the legs and torso. Some focused radiotherapy was delivered under MRI control three times a week for two weeks.

Each time I got closed into the MRI tube for fifty minutes with much clanging and whirring, just before locking me in the nurses would ask if I suffered from claustrophobia. Not yet, was my reply.

By the end of the treatment my legs had returned to their normal size with only some minimal puffiness after walking.

We don't know how long the tumour shrinkage will last or whether further treatment would reverse a recurrence, but right now my legs are both good, real good!

Currently I am on a single intravenou8s treatment given every two weeks which has a cure rate of around 6.7 percent and a partial response of 16.8 percent. Not great odds, but is it better nothing? I don't like to ask.

Shortly after my nolle prosequi, I got a letter from a police inspector in New South Wales about a home death in Phegans Bay. It was a neighbour. After her father-in-law had died, a woman bragged drunkenly that she had pushed her husband to push the subcutaneous doses of drugs to hasten the death. What did I know and was I involved? Eight questions. It happened *six* years ago. And it was a much more complicated story than that. Two weeks after my response via legal aid, the investigation was closed. Was this a warning? Clearly, I thought. How close to death do I need to be, I wondered, to escape further police persecution?

I joined a writing group in the local village during the years on bail. It was a challenge I made to a new friend who was eighty-odd with bad lungs. Let's bring humour into a dreary world and brighten up the village newsletter! She was virtually housebound and I thought a weekly meeting would be good for both of us, get us out. My friend came with me only the once but I continued, quite enjoying the undergraduate feel, half-expecting to be given a novel to be read each week as homework.

The enthusiasm of the conveners was endearing. The tutelage of such a disparate lot would have been daunting, but they struggled on with us. We had lots of laughs and I did curb my adjective use and reduce sentence lengths. I also wrote a tongue-in-cheek article for the local rag on roadkill, but it was never published. Stick to murder!

Every morning I wake to horror. The horror of terminal cancer, often the horror of vomiting as I defecate; often I wake to the horror of nausea that may fade after a vomit or a shit or both. It's not pretty. It's not quiet.

EVIL CONJECTURES

Sometimes the nausea persists. Sometimes the vomiting persists. For hours. I wonder how pregnant women cope. I'm frankly surprised, after a day or so of nausea and vomiting, that the newly knocked-up aren't banging on the obstetrician's door yelling, 'Get it out! Get it out of me!'

Sadly, my cancer is unsuitable for neat excision.

I have forced myself to sift through piles of paper generated by the prolonged investigation. I have looked inside the minds of evil-thinking people keen to share their foul thoughts. I cannot explain the horror of reading the autopsy reports. The indignity of my parents' bodies cut and sliced can be appreciated, but I am left with the horror of what I and others have done for my life to go so horribly wrong. The anguish I have inflicted on others, family bonds strained to breaking point, friendships lost, lies told and death – my get-out-of-jail-free-card, my slap in the face, my constant companion – is invisible but always here, watching, waiting …

Sometimes, when the going is tough, I'm ready to hit the off button. I remember a patient, an old chap, deaf as a post and hard to hear, who told me one day he was ready to let go of the painter. I had never heard the expression before but maybe I did get the gist. It puzzled me enough to mention it to my father. It was while I was working in Hobart and he was a man with considerable boating experience in his youth.

He explained to me that the saying meant letting go of the rope that moors a boat to the jetty: the painter. It meant the old gent was ready to die. I'm sorry I can't finish the story with 'and he died in his sleep a few days later'. I can't recall. There was a time when people often did have a sense of their imminent end. I don't have that yet. I'm too angry to die just yet.

I've learnt not to be frank or honest when people ask how I am. It doesn't do to go into detail and if the true depth of despair is hinted at, I get the suicide-watch calls. Are you OK? No really? Do you want me to come over? 'Please don't!' sounds rude.

I've caused great offence at times by saying I don't want to talk. Of course, it's much better to just not answer the phone on those days when I don't want to lie, when I want to rage or smash something.

They say smashing bottles against a brick wall is useful, but who's going to clean up?

To tell the truth (Ha!) I sometimes wake before dawn and I'll have a dose of morphine and go back to bed so that when I wake up again the sun will be shining and I'll be free of hate, of anger and of horror. I know it's a cheap way out, a too easy solution, a medical balm for a horrible destiny. I only really use it in the mornings, about an hour after waking when stultifying gloom descends like a thick fog, the way it did the day the ute bogged. Some mornings I don't think I'd get out of bed without it. Or I'd be seriously searching for that off button.

So what does that make me? I don't crave the stuff later in the day. I don't exhibit any of the signs of narcotic withdrawal, so I'm not an addict. I've lost my taste for alcohol, so I'm not a drunk – just another emotional cripple trying to survive on the Disability Support Pension.

I wonder, if I got off the morphine and my cancer remained quiescent, I wonder, with the accusation of murder unresolved, if my medical registration could be restored and I could live out my remaining months on some remote Aboriginal outpost where being gay, white and middle-class would not be held against me? Where my mother's death by murder or assisted suicide or recklessness would be nobody's business but mine?

Not Likely. The best I can hope for is to get this story out there so the public can make up their own minds about this menace to society and I can maybe have some financial security before I die and compensate those who have already thrown money into the ring.

A group of lawyers is called an *argument* or an *eloquence*, not a pack of rapacious wolves. Legal fees swallowed $400,000 before we went to legal aid.

I wasn't meant to live this long and (silly me!) I didn't budget for the long term. So, with dwindling savings, it's fun trying to live within the Disability Support Pension. Eating out is out. I live on porridge and stewed fruit, creamed rice, fresh orange juice, fruit salads and green salads; these are things that are cheap and easy for me to prepare and store for that frequent snacking that's needed to prevent further weight loss.

A friend who has helped out in leaner times suggested I use an online charity. Go-fund-me could keep me afloat but what of the media attention? Blow the book, why don't I just go to *Four Corners* with my sad tale or, if I have to, *60 Minutes*, not that that helped Sue Neill-Fraser, another case pursued and won by dear Linda Mason, the woman I refuse to hate.

Eighty percent of cases bought by the prosecution in Tasmania are won. Linda Mason, or the Tasmanian Police have difficulty admitting they're wrong. I've heard Mason is up for a promotion, vying for the bench perhaps. She has avoided losing this case by declaring it over, in the public interest. I think she was avoiding an embarrassing and resounding defeat, but that's just gossip and supposition and, as such, it shouldn't be given it any weight, should it?

Guilty or not, I am, at least, at large. Sue Neill-Fraser's nightmare, on the other hand, is ongoing. The recent prosecution harassment on the stand – of a pregnant and fragile witness in her case – was pathetic to watch. The judge asked for temperance, without any effect. Oh no, the Tasmanian Police are not good at admitting their mistakes.

Some enlightened countries – including Great Britain, Scotland, Canada, Spain, Norway and New Zealand – have formal legal review mechanisms for miscarriages of justice so that they can be examined for lessons to be learnt. My parents called it learning from your mistakes. Those countries with formal review mechanisms also acknowledge the right to compensation after wrongful arrest or prosecution or incarceration. Australia has no such review system in place, despite the country's most disgracefully protracted example. Remember Lindy Chamberlain?

As I write (10 June 2021) several senior figures in the Australian legal community are urging the attorney-general to consider establishing a Criminal Cases Review Commission, 'arguing valid reasons and outlining a practical formula'. The letter was signed by Dr Bob Moles, an esteemed legal academic, researcher and author; the Honourable Michael Kirby; Robert Richter, QC; Ralph Bönig, ex-president of the Law Society of South Australia; Professor Stephen Cordner, former director of the Victorian Institute of Forensic Medicine; and Lara Giddings, a former Tasmanian Premier. If you want to know the statistics on the number of cases referred and overturned in, for example, Britain, two-thirds of the appeals since their review system was set up in 1997 have been allowed. If you want any idea of the truly shocking details, go to thewrongfulconvictionsreport.org and remember the international scandal of Lindy Chamberlain. How long did that last? I don't want to know.

Lately, with a shrinking bank balance, I have taken to eating alone in a number of local food outlets for the disadvantaged. Various kitchens are staffed by do-gooders who dispense fresh food daily; something hot, meaty and vegetarian. They cheerfully dispense comfort food: cottage pie, cauliflower cheese, macaroni cheese, salads, fruit salads, fresh fruit, chunks of watermelon, trifles, apple and rhubarb crumble, bread and butter pudding, day-old pastries and gourmet sandwiches. A company specifically collects food from other companies and outlets to distribute to these free food venues for the needy. Boutique patisseries donate cheesecakes, chocolate gateau, orange poppy seed cake, all of them age well enough. Glacé fruit on French flans glisten enticingly. A toastie of tomato and cheese in yesterday's croissant is a treat. A date scone or fruit bun is great for slicing and toasting later. Such bounty!

In a beanie pulled low and black clothing, I fit right in with the mumbling schizophrenics and more vibrant or agitated members of the disenfranchised. It reminds me of my time in the high-observation ward of prison. I see the same hardened faces, some with tatts creeping up the neck, but now humble, deferential to the hands that feed us with many heartfelt thank-yous. I keep my head down and chew slowly. I hear snippets of conversations about being inside, of getting out. The same old expletives bounce around the courtyard at times but the sun is shining, and not through metal netting. We can walk away.

Two policemen recently swaggered through one such dining area into an inner courtyard and out again looking for someone, with all the arrogance their armed uniforms gave them. My experiences with police and prison guards have left me with a deep hatred of their kind. It's an irrational response I have to sit on. Otherwise, I would be mumbling 'fuck'n pigs' whenever they pass. OK, sometimes I do. Do you think it's fun living with this much anger?

I don't expect to be exonerated or compensated. Basically, I'm fucked. Basically the legal system is fucked. And that is the nineteenth time I have used that word.

I'm hoping to get a rescue dog soon. All that unconditional love and a warm lump on the bed at night.

I get peace through meditation and happiness sitting in a park on sunny afternoons with my sunnies off and my eyes closed for half an hour so that people can tell me how well I look and I can hate them for it. When asked how I am, I say, 'Fine, thanks. And you?'

APPENDICES

One: Medical report prepared by Consultant Forensic Pathologist, **Dr B. Collins**

Two: Medical report prepared by Consultant Physician, **Dr E. Ringrose**

Three: 'On Care of the Elderly Person', by **Dr F. Nicklason**

Four: Character reference by **Dr P. Simpson**

One.

Your ref JFO:1601234.

31 July 2017

Dear Sir,

Re Dr STEPHEN EDWARDS—ats-THE POLICE.

Thank you for referring this case to me for my assessment in relation to the circumstances surrounding and the cause of death of Nelda Mavis EDWARDS.

In preparation of this matter, the Brief materials forwarded with your letter of instruction have been reviewed, with particular reference to the following;

    i   Post-mortem examination report prepared by Forensic Pathologist, Dr D. Ritchey in relation to case no: FP 11972. dated 12/5/2016,

    ii   Toxicology report prepared by Forensic Toxicologist, Ms M. Conner in relation to use no; 1601019 (FP11972),

    iii   Medical report prepared by Forensic Physician, Dr M. Odell dated 21/6/2016,

    iv   Medical report prepared by Palliative Care Specialist, Dr C. Douglas dated 6/9/2016,

    v   Transcript of record of Interview between Dr S. Edwards and Detective Constable Petersen held on 28/4/2016.

In addition, I attended the Office of the State Forensic Pathologist Hobart, Tasmania on 24/7/2017, where I examined a set of 36 light microscope slides, stained *inter alia* with haematoxylin and eosin, which had been prepared from samples of tissues and organs retained by the Pathologist during performance of the autopsy.

It should be noted, that at the time of preparation of this document I have not yet discussed the contents of the autopsy report with Dr Ritchey.

The following are my initial comments and opinions on a number of issues in this case, which may serve as a basis for more detailed explanations with yourself/Counsel, in due course.

1. Whilst I accept that the cause of death as stated in the autopsy report namely "mixed drug toxicity' is reasonable, it obviously relies very heavily on the veracity of the toxicology results, particularly relating to morphine.

2. I agree with Dr Ritchey, that significant natural disease processes identified at autopsy and involving especially the cardiovascular system would have been 'sufficient to account for death in many circumstances'.

3. Examination of the set of fight microscope slides, did not reveal any unidentified pathological condition which could have caused or contributed to the demise, however the extent and severity of the histological abnormalities noted by Dr Richey were clarified.

4. The following significant macroscopic (naked-eye) and microscopic abnormalities were apparent

    i   Old left-sided subdural haemorrhage.

    ii Old ischaemic brain damage – lacunar infarct in corpus striatum.

    iii Bilateral atrial dilation of heart.

    iv Ante-mortem mural thrombus adherent to wall of left atrium.

v   Cortical scars Involving both kidneys.

vi Narrowing of vessels within the myocardium caused by atherosclerosis and amyloid, up to approximately 80% (microscopic examination).

vii Perivascular fibrosis of myocardium (heart muscle).

viii Bilateral nephrosclerosis.

ix Marked venous congestion of the liver.

5. I concur with Dr Ritchey, that thrombotic occlusion of a small intramyocardial vessel with associated ischaemia and infarction of the heart muscle could not be excluded and would not necessarily be Identifiable on microscopic examination of the heart muscle.

6. Seizure associated with old head injury could potentially result in death and should be considered as a possible cause in this case.

7. Biochemical analyses of the vitreous humour showed elevated creatinine (98 μmol/l) and urea (15.0 mmol/l) which are consistent with dehydration and it is interesting to note, that decreased tissue turgor was identified on naked-eye examination of the deceased (p5, autopsy report).

8. In relation to the toxicological analyses of the deceased's autopsy blood sample harvested from a femoral vein, I am concerned that they may not necessarily be representative of the concentrations present at the time of death, because of the well-recognised phenomenon of post-mortem redistribution of drugs, particularly involving morphine, as the post-mortem interval increases.

   In this regard, the Forensic Toxicologist should be questioned as to the reliability of the various concentrations and, whether or not the blood morphine concentration of 0.3 mg/l could have actually been lower and, possibly, within the therapeutic/non-toxic range.

9. If it were agreed, that all the drug concentrations were within the range of accepted therapy, then this would decrease any weight which could be given to the role of drug toxicity in the death of Mrs Edwards.

10. The pharmacokinetic of some drugs in this case are as follows:

   a   Morphine   Blood half-life: 1-8 hours.

   b   Midazolam   Blood half-life: 1.5-2.5 hours.

   c   Clonazepam   Blood half-life: 20-80 hours

   d   Oxazepam   Blood half-life: 4-15 hours.

I trust these précis comments have been of assistance and I look forward to discussing the matter further at conference, after which I would be pleased to provide a supplementary report, if necessary.

Yours faithfully,

Dr R. Byron Collins,

Consultant Forensic Pathologist,

INDEPENDENT FORENSIC SERVICES.

Two.

Dr Edward Ringrose, MB., B.S., F.R.A.C.P.

Suite 30, Level 2

CONSULTANT PHYSICIAN

Silverton Place, 101 Wickham Terrace Brisbane QId 4000

T 073831 56811 F 07 3831 5682

www.lexlmed.com.auj ABN 6036766914-4

15 September 2017

Dear Mr O'Shannessey, Murdoch Clarke Lawyers GPO Box 408, HOBART TAS 7001

In the Matter of: Dr Stephen Edwards

Your Reference:]FO:JFO: 1601234

Date of File Review: 1 September 2017

Consultant Physician Dr Edward Ringrose, MB., B.S., F.R.A.C.l'

QUALIFICATIONS & FELLOWSHIPS

H   Bachelor of Medicine and Bachelor of Surgery

H   Fellow of the Royal Australasian College of Physicians

AREAS OF EXPERTISE

Diseases of the Endocrine System – U disorders of the Internal (endocrine) glands such as the thyroid and adrenal glands, disorders such as diabetes, metabolic and nutritional disorders, obesity, pituitary diseases

I,   Disease of the Gastrointestinal System – V.

diagnosis and treatment of diseases of the digestive organs including the stomach, bowels, liver and gall bladder. This specialist treats conditions such as abdominal pain, ulcers, diarrhoea, cancer and jaundice

$1   Chronic Fatigue Syndrome   U

re   Kidney Disease - diagnosis and treatment of U

disorders of the kidney, high blood pressure, fluid and mineral balance

U   Pain Management

SUMMARY

Diseases of the Nervous System - diagnosis and treatment of all types of disease or impaired function of the brain, spinal cord, peripheral nerves, muscles and autonomic nervous system.

Respiratory Medicine – diagnosis and treatment of cancer, pneumonia, pleurisy, asthma,   occupational and environmental diseases, bronchitis, sleep disorders, emphysema and other complex disorders of the lungs and respiratory system.

Infectious Diseases

Cardiac Disease – diagnosis and treatment of diseases of the heart and blood vessels including abnormal heartbeat rhythms and hypertension.

Dr Edward Ringrose has extensive experience in the diagnosis and treatment of medical conditions in patients with psychiatric illnesses.

POSITIONS

Private Practice - Brisbane H   Current Hospital Affiliations

- The Wesley Hospital, Auchenflower
- Brisbane Private Hospital, Spring Hill
- Toowong Private Hospital, Toowong
- New Farm Clinic, New Farm

H   Consultant Physician

- Nambour
- Longreach
- Mount Isa

U   Chair of Q-COMP Medical Assessment Tribunal

H   Member of Council and for twelve years Honorary Secretary of the Medical Defence Society of Queensland

In response to your request dated 5 September 2017, I am providing an Independent File Review on the matter of Dr Stephen Edwards. I am aware of the Uniform Civil Procedure Rules 1999 and I have complied with Rules 426, 427 and 428.

DOCUMENTS PROVIDED:

I note the following documents have been provided to me for this file review:

a) Letter of request and terms of reference for report

b) Schedule of specific questions

c) Copy of relevant medical and claim file information.

DOCUMENT REVIEW:

I reviewed the documents made available to me prior to completing this Independent File Review.

SPECIFIC QUESTIONS:

In reply to your schedule of specific question, I can offer the following responses:

1. Your qualifications for giving an opinion in this case. Details of your past experience in treating patients in palliative care setting and your experience with the medications administered in this case.

I am a Consultant Physician, a Fellow of the Royal Australian College of Physicians.

I have practised internal medicine at a specialist level for approximately fifty years.

I was employed for many years as a part time Visiting Specialist to a number of hospitals in Queensland and I had an extensive private practice in Brisbane with constant care of inpatients in private hospitals.

For all of my working life I have covered a wide range of illnesses, being a general physician. This involved extensive inpatient care in private and public hospitals. A great deal of the work was involved in caring for people in their older years. This included care of people with cerebrovascular accidents, major cardiac problems, renal failure et cetera. Many of these patients were admitted to hospital in a terminal condition and it was my role to look after them as they died. I would have, over this long period, cared for hundreds of people in this situation.

When it was obvious that people were going to die it was my role to make sure that they did not suffer at all during their dying days. This involved the use of medications similar to those outlined in this case as well as the medications used on Ms Edwards. It is my opinion that it is the role of the doctor caring for such patients to be sure that they do not suffer in their dying days. The use of drugs similar to those used in this case is mandatory in the conduct of a person dying to ensure that they do not suffer unnecessarily. Sometimes one has to use what would be regarded as large doses to achieve this end.

In the course of my practice I have extensive experience with the use of morphine and other narcotic agents, midazolam, clonazepam, Serepax and many other such agents.

2. What you understand to be the facts upon from which your opinion is based, including the range of possible doses of medication and their administration.

I shall outline fairly extensively what I regard as the significant facts in this case.

Firstly it is important to outline the conditions from which Ms Edwards suffered. I shall outline these giving my own opinion of their nature and also when required I will have referred to the text Harrison's Principles of Internal Medicine, a respected textbook of internal medicine.

The conditions from which Ms Edwards suffered are as follows:

- Myelodysplasia: Myelodysplasia covers a heterogeneous group of haematological disorders. These can affect red blood cells, white blood cells and platelets. Most patients with this condition die as a result of complications of pancytopaenia, diminution of all these cells. The prognosis for this condition is extremely poor. Life expectancy when it is diagnosed varies from a few months to a few years. Cytotoxic drugs may help in its treatment however it is not a curable condition.

- Multiple fractures from falls: Ms Edwards fractured her L5 vertebra in 2010 and then in 2014 suffered three fractures, of the left humerus, acetabulum and olecranon.

- Cervical spondylosis, significant arthritis of the cervical spine.

- Vascular dementia.

- Rectal adenocarcinoma in 2012: This was a multifocal tumour with recurrences and was preceded by a number of tubulovillous adenomas.

- Hypertension.

- In 2006 Ms Edwards suffered a transient cerebral ischaemic attack and was found to have neutropaenia.

- In 2015 she suffered a cerebrovascular accident, stroke, and this resulted in expressive and receptive dysphasia. It was also accompanied by insomnia and incoordination.

- Computed Tomography (CT) Scans of the brain in 2007 and 2011 were reported as showing age related atrophic changes, that is shrinkage of the brain, moderate cerebral atrophy with dilated ventricles. Her symptoms at this time included blurred vision, and problems with memory and calculation.

- Atrial fibrillation.

- In August 2014 at the Royal Hobart Hospital she was admitted with the fractures set out above, an acute confusional state, and a subdural haematoma requiring emergency neurosurgery followed by a reasonable recovery. After this however she had epileptic seizures and expressive dysphasia.

- In October 2014 a Computed Tomography (CT) Scan of the brain showed extensive degeneration of the brain. There were extensive hypodensities in the periventricular and deep white matter, generalised atrophic changes and prominent ventricles; in February 2015 she fell backwards at home and this is when she fractured the neck of her right femur. At that time the hospital staff had concerns about her cognitive function and her ability to live independently.

In July 2014 a letter from Dr Edwards, her son, to Dr Elizabeth Brown, General Practitioner, asking Dr Brown to be the family general practitioner stated that his father had Alzheimer's disease, and his mother had multi-infarct dementia and transient ischaemic attacks. He stated that both had little insight into their conditions.

Dr David Dunbabin, Consultant Physician, in April 2015 after the treatment for the fractured femur, stated Ms Edwards had a period of agitated delirium on a background of cognitive impairment, fails and subdural haematoma. He also stated in March 2016 to the Coroner's Office, "I believe her dependence on her husband and her cognitive impairment would have made her susceptible to suggestion by a loved one or a member of the family. She was heavily dependent on her husband."

Other facts which are relevant to this case are that Ms Edwards had a son who died on 20 February 2016 in Thailand. After this in the form of a statutory declaration Dr Jonathon Smith, General Practitioner Locum, stated that he spoke to Ms Edwards after the death of her son and that she asked for an injection to kill her. He of course refused.

An affidavit by Dr Edwards on 4 March 2016 stated that on 1 March 2016 he flew from Sydney. His father died the next day, 2 March 2016 and he found out that his mother had not been drinking or eating for a number of days. At that time she would only drink sips of water that he gave her. He pointed out that his brother Glendon had died on 20 February 2016 and then his father David on 2 March 2016.

There is also evidence that when her husband was dying Ms Edwards refused to take her regular medication because she wanted also to die. She suffered from severe hypertension.

I shall now summarise the information I have gleaned about Ms Edwards' final few days.

The second day after her husband died, Ms Edwards did not eat or drink other than having a brandy and dry. The third day after his death she was up and out of bed and dressed because people were coming to visit however she did not drink and went to bed at 5:00pm. On the fourth day after her husband died she was described as being hysterical and this is when Dr Edwards gave her some clonazepam at 10:00am and then stated she stopped moving around the bed with an irregular rapid heart rate and irregular respirations. It was at this time he thought she was dying and to make sure she was not suffering he gave her some morphine and midazolam.

I should say at this point that it is very difficult to determine how much morphine had been given. I have been through the record of the police interview with Dr Edwards on a couple of occasions and it is difficult to know just how much morphine was given by Dr Edwards. Other information from that interview sets out that he was asked why he did no tests on his mother. The answer was that he decided she was dying because of her pulse and respiratory rates and did not think testing was required. Personally in my opinion this was a sensible decision. His mother wanted to die, she had expressed that wish in the past and she did not want any medical intervention.

There was a history of Ms Edwards having made a conscious decision not to eat or drink and she had threatened suicide previously.

Returning to the interview, on Page 124 there is some discussion of morphine dosages and it was stated, I believe by the police officer, that to an opiate naive person the dose should be 2.5 milligrams of morphine and not 10 milligrams. At this stage I would state that I disagree with this. If morphine is being given to a dying person to reduce suffering it is reasonable to use 10 milligrams which is not a large dose of morphine. I also disagree with the suggestion that the doses of clonazepam were excessive. With someone in this situation and in particular an eighty-eight-year-old female with a multiplicity of diseases that are not curable, it is reasonable to be sure that they do not suffer as they are dying. To do this sometimes it is necessary to use more than the suggested doses of drugs to be sure the patient is not suffering. When death is inevitable the patient must be comfortable at all times.

3. *Your opinion as to the cause of death of Ms Nelda Edwards.*

In my opinion the causes of Ms Edwards' death were as follows:

- Renal failure: Ms Edwards' fluid intake over the week or so prior to death was negligible from the information provided. She was eighty-eight years of age and her renal function would have rapidly deteriorated with inadequate fluid intake.

- Myelodysplasia: As stated above this is a serious, terminal illness for which there is no significant therapy.

- Cerebrovascular disease: There is significant evidence of widespread cerebral degeneration undoubtedly due to arterial problems in a person of advanced age.

- Severe hypertension.

- Atrial fibrillation.

4. *Your opinion as to whether the administration of medication to Ms Nelda Edwards by Dr Stephen Edwards was appropriate by reasonable palliative care standards.*

Initially I would state that in my opinion Dr Edwards should have recorded the dosages of the various drugs that he gave his mother. Some of the doses appear to be slightly larger than recommended however in my experience this is not a fault. The whole principle of alleviating suffering in a dying person is to make sure they are not suffering. In my opinion Ms Edwards' death was inevitable. As set out above she had a series of serious illnesses over a period and this was compounded by her refusal to take food or fluids for a significant period prior to her death and the refusal to take her medication. It is possible Dr Edwards gave doses that would normally be regarded as greater than should have been administered. However, in alleviating the suffering of a patient, one does not necessarily use the doses that are said to be correct. As I have stated above, the overall important factor in someone dying with such an extensive medical history is that they must not suffer at all. Sometimes to be sure that this course is undertaken it is necessary to give doses that would in other situations be regarded as excessive. The dying person must not be allowed to suffer.

It is also my opinion that it would have been wiser for Dr Edwards to have enlisted the assistance of another doctor at this time. However, this was not done and that was his decision.

In summary, it is my opinion that although the dosages of the medications were large, they were appropriate in the circumstances of the death of Ms Edwards.

SPECIFIC UNDERTAKINGS:

I am aware of the Uniform Civil Procedure Rules governing the provision of expert witness reports. I have complied with those rules and I recognise my duty to the court.

- The factual matters stated in the report are, as far as I know, true.
- I have made all enquiries considered appropriate.
- The opinions stated in the report are genuinely held by me.
- The report contains references to all matters I consider significant.

Yours sincerely

DR EDWARD W. RINGROSE

On Care of the Elderly Person

Medical care of elderly people, especially the frail elderly, has the aim of maintaining quality of life, dignity, functional status, and role in family and society.

1) These aims are best achieved by comprehensive geriatric assessment (CGA) and carefully tailored interventions based on problems identified which are impacting adversely on quality of life, dignity, function, and role.

CGA involves careful evaluation of the patient's medical history noting both active and inactive problems, drug therapy and previous treatments and the effects, positive and negative, of these treatments.

Cognitive and physical function requires specific consideration. Cognitive function assessment requires a detailed informant history coupled with objective and validated tests of cognition. Examples of such objective tests are the Mini Mental State Examination and the Montreal Cognitive Assessment. When assessing cognitive function, deficits in hearing, depressed mood, personality factors, life experiences and education, psychosis, dysphasia, delirium, and non-fluency in English must be considered as potential confounding influences.

In assessing-physical function, basic activities of daily living (BADL) and instrumental activities of daily living (IADL) are examined. BADLs include mobility and continence. IADLs include cooking and using a telephone.

Finally in a CGA the social circumstances in which an elderly person lives are assessed. Amongst other things evaluation of key supports and deficits in support systems is undertaken.

2) The key health professional in the care of an elderly person is the General Practitioner (GP). Often the GP will have a detailed understanding, with longitudinal perspective, of the elderly person, their medical history, family, personality, values, interests, and fears. GPs frequently develop a care plan for their patients who have complex needs. These plans have a problem list and treatment goals. The plans also have the names of other specialists involved in the care of the patient.

When there is frailty and/or medical complexity then the GP may seek the assessment and opinion of a Geriatrician. A Geriatrician may be able to assist with the diagnosis of cognitive impairment (including assessment of mental competence and advanced care planning), disorders affecting gait and balance, requirement for rehabilitation or, more generally, medical assessment and management in the face of frailty and complexity. Geriatricians may be involved in acute care of the frail elderly in hospital settings. In acute settings the Geriatrician pays particular care to identify iatrogenesis (such as adverse drug reactions) and other hazards of hospitalisation. The Geriatrician also ensures that an adequate history of base-line functional status (mental and physical) has been obtained and that the social context of the patient is thoroughly understood.

3) The comprehensive assessment and management of frail elderly people with complex care needs involves input from a range of allied health professionals. These include physiotherapist, occupational therapist, speech therapist, social workers, and nurses (and others according to need). Corroborative information is required in the assessment phase from other family members/friends/advocates in situations where there is cognitive impairment. Corroborative history is mandatory if there is any question of unreliability of the information given by the elderly person themself. The input of family members/friends/advocates can be crucial in the success of implementation care plans developed by the multidisciplinary team. The GP is a key member of the multidisciplinary team caring for an elderly person with complex care needs. Frequently the GP performs crucial co-ordination and communication functions.

4) In general a referral to access comprehensive multidisciplinary geriatric medical care is required from a GP. Effective geriatric services recognise that some frail and isolated elderly people may no longer have a relationship with a GP. In this circumstance a family member or community

service provider may alert the Aged Care Assessment Team and/or a Geriatric Service that there is an elderly person at risk who needs an assessment of needs. Attempts are then made to identify a GP who is willing to accept this person for ongoing care.

5) The purpose of CGA is to identify health and social needs and to develop a plan to address those needs as best as is possible. Sometimes there is resistance from the elderly person regards the recommendations of the plan. Resistance may arise in the setting of personality characteristics, life experiences, cognitive impairment or other factors. The GP must be made aware of the treatment plan that has been developed and therefore be given opportunity to modify the plan if necessary or at least discuss the details of the plan. Family members are invited to contribute information to develop the plan and may request a copy of the plan. If an elderly person loses the capacity to make competent decisions in the face of threatening problems such as health risk, domestic or driving incompetence then guardianship discussions may be necessary. A guardian may be appointed to make decisions in the interests of the incompetent person in the setting of identified risk. Adequate assessment of competence to make a particular decision is a core competency of Geriatricians and Old Age Psychiatrists. Prior to formal assessment of competence it is assumed that a person retains competence.

6) The plan for the care of an elderly person will often evolve as the identified needs and resulting risks change. Members of the multidisciplinary team provide evidence of changing needs to the family, GP, and Geriatrician. This evidence forms the basis for plan modifications. It is essential that newly identified problems are reported efficiently to the GP and the patient's family in a written form.

7) Because elderly people often have a variety of medical conditions, they may be seeing a variety of medical doctors in addition to the GP. Best practice is that when new conditions are diagnosed and new doctors are involved in care then information is shared with all the treating doctors so that all the doctors are aware of the other doctors involved and their role. Geriatricians frequently have a role in integrating information from the GP and other specialists and helping formulate an overall plan based on patient preferences, family wishes, what is possible medically possible, and what is practical in the social circumstances that exist.

8) I have described best practice above. Inevitably in medicine, as in life in general, breakdowns occur in communication. Communication breakdowns are at the root of most instances of suboptimal medical care. These breakdowns occur for a variety of reasons. Breakdowns especially occur at times when there is a sudden change in health care needs, when decisions need to be made rapidly, or if there is fragmentation of care between different providers, e.g., public and private services. Breakdowns can occur when family members have fundamentally different opinions about what represents appropriate care for their relative.

9) In Tasmania geriatricians and other service providers for elderly people try to reduce fragmentation of care by seeking corroborative information from important others: family members, community service providers etc. There is a concerted effort to ensure appropriate documentation and communication of assessments and care plans.

10) It is a principle that doctors/nurses should not treat family members except in exceptional circumstances as judgement can be clouded by emotional and other factors.

Three.

Dr Frank Nicklason, FRACP,

Staff Specialist Physician

Head, Department of Geriatric Medicine, RHH

27/9/2016

23 July 2016

The Presiding Judge, The Supreme Court, Hobart Tasmania.

Your Honour,

I have been asked by the solicitors instructed by Dr Stephen Edwards if I would provide a character reference for him. The solicitors have explained to me the charges Stephen is facing and the fact he is on remand in jail in Tasmania. As I now live in Queensland, I have not been able to speak directly to him. However, I am happy to provide Stephen such a reference as I have a great deal of respect and admiration for him.

Prior to my moving to Queensland in December last year, I had worked with Stephen as my principal associate in General Practice in Woy Way, New South Wales, for a period of some four years. Since 2002 I also have worked as a medicolegal adviser to one of Australia's major medical indemnity insurance providers, assisting them to setup their NSW operations. As a result, I am very aware of my duty to the Court and what I state in this reference I would be prepared to give as sworn evidence.

In 2012 Stephen moved from Tasmania to the Central Coast of NSW, where he had previously worked as a junior doctor at the Gosford District Hospital. He moved there with the intention of setting up a private practice to care for the aged of our community, especially those within nursing homes. He approached me to see if he could base himself out of my rooms and this is how the association developed.

Stephen was dedicated to this task and within a short period was medically responsible for the majority of the aged out-of-home care in our community. He provided personal on-call medical care seven days a week and as required at any time of the day or night. I admired and respected him for that and the care I personally observed him provide was of a very high standard. I sometimes provided back up for him when he was out of area, but even then he usually took his own telephone advice calls in the first instance as he knew the patients so well. He showed a real concern and genuine respect for them. In return Stephen provided cover for my patients two days a week when I was on full-time duty in my medicolegal capacity in Sydney. The association worked well.

During our time at the practice there were several occasions where I had the opportunity to observe first-hand his attitude towards his parents and his concern for them. If required, he would fly down at short notice to ensure they were coping and to provide any assistance they needed. He never begrudged them this time and never expressed anything other than love for them. He appeared very genuine in this regard.

I do not know what else I can say. I believe Stephen is a very principled person. He has applied for bail, and from my knowledge of him I would support that application despite the seriousness of the charge against him. I believe that any conditions applied to that ball would be strictly adhered to.

It is difficult in a reference such as this to cover all the issues that might be applicable. I would be more than happy to speak to the reference if required or to answer any questions the Court may have.

Yours sincerely

Peter Simpson, MB RS FRACGP DRANZCOG

Dr Peter Simpson, 72 Monterey Keys Drive, Helensvale QLD 4212

PHOTOGRAPHS

Nelda Edwards 1948

Stephen, David, Robert, Leigh, Nelda and Glendon, 1962

Nelda models her new handbag on the banks of the Murray River, 1965.

Graduation Day.
Mother confided her buttons could have burst.

David and Nelda, in 2008, enjoying one of
their cruises. Guess who made the blouse.

On a cruise 2012

David and Nelda visited Oman on a 2009 cruise and met up with Glendon. Another self-made blouse.

Stephen, the author, recently.

THE STORIES

PREAMBLE

In some bucolic retirement I had imagined collecting all the stories I have written over the years as nurse and doctor and publishing them in two small volumes, one a mostly upbeat collection and another more sombre collection concerning death as part of the death education movement. This is a recent development designed to stimulate discussion around the dying process and how it is organised in our medicalised world.

I became involved in the local movement, helping out with coffee and cake and death education. The level of public interest and misinformation illustrated the need for this sort of informed but informal discussion. This does not make me a euthanasia proponent, rather someone who believes that death has been over medicalised. We have lost the art of death and easy access to dying with dignity.

The publishers wanted the following collection of stories included to add meaning to *my* story, where this book started. This collection and more were appropriated by the police as part of the investigation, so I hope they found them interesting. Sadly – for the prosecution found them helpful in establishing a motive of euthanasia.

Everyone is dying but few of us give it much thought. Most people imagine fading out politely in their own homes but in Australia only seventeen per cent of us manage to die outside of a medical institution. It's nicer that way for nice white families who generally manage pretty badly if the going gets tough or even when a smooth end is nigh.

It seems that, unlike the Chinese, Indians, Muslims or Aborigines, we've lost the art of caring for the dying. A hundred years ago old people would often sense when their end was imminent and invite the nearest and dearest over for a celebration. If the dying process was prolonged, death-bed vigils were rostered amongst family and the village. Children would visit, laughter and tears were shared, possessions passed on, last words uttered.

Having worked in hospitals, hospices, nursing homes and private homes as a nurse and doctor for many years now, this author is more familiar with death than most. Here are some real end-of-life tales that may prompt a moment's consideration of the inevitable before we find ourselves, perhaps with no warning, at death's door.

THE LOOK OF DEATH

ON NEEDING to share this tale, the doctor is at pains to make it plain that no self-aggrandisement is intended. The short and recent factual events related here will not, he hopes, be seen as how-smart-am-I stories but taken as they are intended; startling warnings of how far out of touch with death Western society has become.

As women now still develop cravings for what their inner nutritional needs are during pregnancy, only a hundred years ago and for eons before, people often felt some personal intuition of imminent demise, an inner sense of impending death now mostly lost in a system where further treatment and cure is always an option. Once, not long ago, it was not unusual for family and friends to be invited to a final farewell a weekend before. By invitations or word of mouth, people would gather for some final celebration of a life before the body would be found, only days later, wearing an expression of great peace.

Faces change as death approaches. The slow loss of weight quickens and this is especially obvious in the face which suddenly becomes more drawn and gaunt. Consciousness comes and goes. Startling periods of lucidity may appear in the demented. Often, in the final days, the dying go through an indescribable transformation and shortly before – or even at the point of – death, the face assumes an expression of great beauty and bliss. Commonly, family members comment on how peaceful they look.

Most people, those who do not die of some sudden catastrophe but have suffered some long and lingering death, go through this period of profound, even transcendental change. Family rifts from distant disputes are quickly resolved in floods of tears. A sense of completeness is felt; facial creases melt away as if all of life's myriad worries have been left behind. Some days or hours before the failing heart and lungs together call it quits and breathing ceases, the face settles into an expression of startlingly beatific smiling serenity.

In some Indian religions, as death approaches, the devotees forgo food and fluid and find some final place of repose to die a few days later; like cats or dogs, who also have a far better developed sense of death than modern man. The growth of cities and sanitisation of death means that children no longer confront the horror of a chicken running around with its head cut off, as chickens do for a few minutes. Chicken is fried or wrapped in plastic. Eggs come in cardboard cartons. Pets grow old and then disappear to the vets. Old people go into homes or hospitals. No longer does the village organise a roster for deathbed vigils with the old matriarch or patriarch propped up on many pillows, delivering final words of love and advice to a weeping family as small children and pets run in and out. No longer does the demented grandmother sit in the inglenook by the fire shelling peas or rocking the latest baby, crooning senselessly, fading away until a cough carries her off in the night.

Now the family demand the best treatment for their ailing mother: antibiotics and white hospital sheets and overworked nurses to keep things clean, and doctors to deliver a modicum of pain relief when the antibiotics fail, and then more drugs to dry up the distressing-to-the-family death rattle in the final hours. This is modern death.

So back to the story, the look of death.

The doctor was sitting in a nurses' station to the side of the main living room area of a residential aged care facility where people entered as low-care, mostly independent residents and then progressed at various speeds through various stages of declining physical or mental health, where different combinations of decrepitude and dementia determine the in-house moves to either high care or more secure accommodation as the mind and body wander.

In mild dementia the mind goes a little soft around the edges, a bit vague about the fine detail. It can last like that for many years, only slowly deepening until the rapid decline into severe dementia begins, now termed 'advanced' so as not to alarm the relatives as much. It's gaga-land to the extent that family may receive abuse or not be recognised as kin, confronted by incoherence or mute absence.

As people move through the different areas within the same residential complex, it is charmingly described as *aging in place*. Single rooms, bigger living rooms, more carpet; it costs a little more and looks much nicer than more understaffed hostel and nursing home options. Doctors are mostly obliged by prevailing attitudes to deliver antibiotics to keep the final cough at bay, and in all these facilities the nurses continue to turn and wash and feed a huge and mostly abandoned population of deeply demented and bedbound souls lost on a lonely voyage towards a long-postponed death, marooned in some in-between place, the tears and crying-out remedied by antidepressants and psychotropic drugs, with tranquillisers and sedatives to maintain day and night in a parody of care. There they lie, locked in death's waiting room where family and friends visit regularly or not – mostly not.

In the large living room of such an establishment, the doctor found himself examining a new resident just arrived from the local hospital ready for 'admission'. He leaned over the trolley sides to briefly feel for her thready pulse and watch her breathing while offering pleasantries. She was thin and very old. Unspeaking, her eyes opened to look past him to some distant place far away. The heavily wrinkled skin seemed to fall from her face as her eyes closed again. She had the look of death.

The ambulance attendants and nurses seemed unconcerned as she was settled into a bed.

The doctor examined the pages of the discharge summary which had arrived with her from the hospital. No mention of dying. Various fractures and other complications had been successfully treated to return the old lady from the brink of delirium and death, after a fall, to a comfortable condition in which, although too frail to be rehabilitated and safely returned to her home, and in the absence of any family willing to drop everything and come to her aid, she could only be safely moved to a residential aged care facility providing full-time nursing, cleaning and food-producing services.

It looked great on paper but the person in the trolley was dying. I stopped all the oral tablets. The time for cholesterol reduction was long past. The nurses were unable to feed her anything or get her to drink. After a day, I asked them to stop trying and called the family. She died a few days later.

The second occasion related to this story occurred in a transitional care unit, a step-down facility akin to the old-time convalescent homes for old people recovering from fractures, operations, strokes or other calamities where the initial injury had been stabilised in hospital and they are ready for slow rehabilitation and then discharge to either some sort of supported home care or the dreaded nursing home placement.

The case in point arrived late in the day. She was tall and gaunt, a woman of great age and little if any mental decline; she had preserved an acerbic sense of humour. When the doctor arrived, an old and experienced nurse, fond of bossing him around in a kindly fashion, pulled him aside and with a pointed look asked him to see this lady *now*. As they walked down a corridor, the sister listed the afflictions stabilised by the hospital, but only as they were almost upon her did the sister say, 'And she is still not eating or drinking anything.'

I looked down at her emaciated figure. Her hearing was very poor and her Scottish brogue thick, so conversation wasn't easy; but after a lot of yelling, it was clear she was in no discomfort and had no desire for food or fluid. The sister and doctor looked up from her and their eyes met. When they left the room and were walking back along the corridor to the nurses' station, the sister had the courtesy to wait for the doctor to say it first.

'She's dying.'

As it happened, the sister had also worked in palliative care and had more than the usual experience of death. The funny thing was, the two of them had a hard time convincing the rest of the not entirely young team of dedicated and experienced physiotherapists, occupational therapists, registered nurses, a case manager and a ward manager that the woman was, indeed, dying. A reference to recent decreased appetite was then found in the notes from the hospital. She resolutely refused to eat and only sipped a little water or warm tea from the most determined nurses as she lay in her bed decrying all attempts at joining in any activities with other residents.

Over the next few days, it was increasingly clear that she would soon be gone. Strangely, the sister and doctor continued to have the greatest difficulty convincing some of the staff of the same. The two sons were especially disbelieving. They reported how the hospital had done such a wonderful job of putting their mother back together. She had been so well. Nothing had been mentioned about dying. Surely the doctor was wrong. What new drug was needed? Which specialist should be consulted?

A bustling rehabilitation ward is no place to die comfortably. One needs peace and quiet as the transformation takes place. The doctor managed to get her into a nursing home nearby where her two sons sat, each holding a hand and denying her death, until it arrived a few days later.

DORIS

DORIS LIVED high, high up on the very top floor of tall building within a convent complex erected long ago and enclosed behind a high brick wall that skirted a bend in the bank of the river. Perhaps Doris knew this once, years ago when she arrived. Large windows looked out across the river and serried roofs beyond but inside it was all wipe-down Laminex- or vinyl-covered furniture with a bustling team of nurses, a few nuns, a cook and a cleaner to care for Doris and fifteen other very, very old people in varying states of advanced decrepitude amongst the dusty plastic plants and constant TV.

Lovingly washed and fed three times a day by the aging religious sisters devoted to their work and the brash and brisk state registered nurses, the mumbling or mute patients were moved each day from bed to armchair to bed again, indifferent to the bells calling the nuns to worship or the clouds gathering in the sky outside and reflecting darkly in the river below as it ran quietly by to some unavoidable appointment under the Sydney Harbour Bridge with the ocean beyond.

Some old folks go quietly but others throw rocks into these calm pools of contemplation. Doris was one of those who complained loudly.

'Jack, Jack!' she would call angrily, over and over again. 'Where are you, Jack?' she would cry, looking around blindly, clawing weakly at the worn vinyl arms of the armchair that conspired by its depth to keep her against her will. After an anguished time, Doris would fall back hopelessly into the chair's embrace and slumber awhile in medicated stupor until the next wash or turn or spoonful.

The others residents seemed more accepting of their fate. Some even picked up the sense of urgency when the nurses were preparing for a 'round', getting things set to rights before Mother Superior arrived with the doctor. Feeding bibs were quickly removed, matching slippers retrieved and dressing gowns rearranged more decorously. When the double doors swung open and the sisters stood to attention by the charts, Doris called out loudly,

'Jack, Jack, is that you?'

As a nurse moved to pat her shoulder the doctor murmured

'Perhaps some more Serepax?' as he moved on. 'Can't have her upsetting the rest.'

The sisters smiled in obeisance. Over the next few days Doris's calls to Jack became fainter and further apart but no less desperate. The new registered nurse felt her heart torn by Doris's calls and decided on an experiment. The Serepax, an old-style sedative known to increase confusion and falls, was furtively flushed down the sink. The nurse began yelling back into Doris's better ear.

'Jack's not here. It's Rachel.'

'Who?' Doris screeched.

'Rachel. It's Rachel, what do you want?'

'Where's Jack, I want Jack,' Doris yelled back, but the nurse persisted, day after day.

'Jack's not here, it's Rachel, what do you want' running through the basic list of food, drink, and toileting. It took a few weeks and a lot of flushed Serepax before Doris stopped calling for Jack and started calling for Rachel instead. Doris began adding requests for more of this or that. Her wrinkled forehead smoothed a little and sometimes she seemed almost to smile at the smell of tea and toast. No-one complained when Doris started murmuring, 'Thank you, dear' when blanket and pillows were adjusted.

As her face became calmer the suggestion of a smile became clearer. Occasionally she would sing snatches of old dance tunes that would cause the nurses to pause between changing channels on the TV. Doris started calling for Rachel, who would hurry to her side. I'm here Doris, what can I do for you my darling? Can you hear the bells? Would you like a cup of tea and a biscuit now?

Rachel finally and with great trepidation admitted her medication omissions regarding Doris to her employers. The sisters seemed unconcerned. Doris had become quietly spoken and appreciative of the pillow-patting and cups of tea. Strangely though, once Doris had attained her new state of peace her interest in tea and cake diminished. When it was clear she was dying she remained in her room and her snatches of Nat King Cole were replaced by fragments of hymns and Hail Marys echoed in unison with the nuns who gathered around Doris, never leaving her side as she drifted on her own river with surprising speed and great calm towards the bridge between life and death.

One day, though a busy shift, Rachel felt drawn to check on Doris a few times. The low chanting of the nuns filled the room with a feeling of peace. Doris seemed transformed, her face radiant, deeply asleep and hardly bothering to breathe but still lingering here on earth.

At the end of her shift, instead of rushing to her car, Rachel went to a door she had found in the tall brick wall that surrounded the convent buildings. After a struggle with rusty bolts and chains and a bit of push and shove, the door yielded and Rachel found herself brushing through some weeds to find a grassy spot to sit with her back to the wall.

Pulling off her shoes, Rachel rolled herself a cigarette, thinking about Doris as she watched the big fat river flowing past indifferently just beyond her feet. How much longer will she float between life and death Rachel wondered, not knowing until the next day that it was just about then that Doris chose to the leave this mortal coil.

THE CAT STRUCK BACK

THE MAN HAD been close to death for some time. Trips to and from hospital had long ceased. Part of the brain had been removed but the cancer returned. Radiotherapy had been used to shrink further advances of the cancer until the battle was declared lost and palliative care was the final option.

Brain cancers seem to strike men in their early fifties, which is all the more tragic for the widows-in-waiting who watch the dreams of years ahead disintegrate before their eyes. He had been a hard-working man and a loving husband and father. The house sat high on hill overlooking a bay. The wife and daughters supported each other as the doctor slowly increased medication to control the headaches and temper. The surgery, the cancer and the radiotherapy had all contributed to a marked mental decline and personality change. With frontal lobe damage people become a little punch-drunk, disinhibited and belligerent at times. The women managed his wilful outbursts as mothers do with bad tempered children; distracting him, offering food and looking after the medication.

One day, towards the end, the doctor was called to check a new wound. In a moment left alone slumbering in his chair, he was jumped on by the family cat, which scratched a bare arm from the shoulder to hand. Would he need antibiotics, what should be done?

The scratch was certainly impressive but not deep. The wife was distraught. The old cat was a family favourite never given to such behaviour. The cat sat in a sunny living room window cleaning her paws as she watched the doctor and women tending to the now mostly slumbering man. Antiseptic, non-stick dressings and crepe bandages were applied. The cat was picked up by the wife and scolded. She purred loudly as the doctor stroked her.

'She has never scratched anyone,' the wife declared, obviously distressed. 'The girls used to dress her in doll's clothes when they were little.'

'How did she get on with your husband?' asked the doctor.

'Not so well,' she said, looking down at the cat still in her arms.

'Dad hated that cat.' The daughter present added quietly.

'Really?'

'Oh yes. He was always pushing her off the living room armchairs and shooing her outside.

Said he was allergic, though he never showed it.'

'Oh, well, I suggest you keep the cat out of this room if he is alone again.'

The women were mortified. The cat continued purring and looked up adoringly.

The call came, late at night a few weeks later. The breathing, the groaning, can you come soon? The doctor did all he could to ease the way until, just before dawn the laboured breathing ceased and the furrowed brow relaxed. The scratch wounds had scabbed up nicely without infection. Neat rows of tiny vengeful scabs had all fallen away only a few days earlier, leaving no trace behind.

They moved to the kitchen to make tea as the sun rose. The old cat greeted them warmly.

MRS GREEN

OLIVE AND ROGER Green had been coming to the clinic for some time. Now in their eighties, Olive was always well presented and delicately deferential. Her subtle management of her increasingly frail and profoundly deaf husband was a pleasure to watch when they attended for routine scripts or licence renewals. In mauve-tinted helmet of perfectly coiffured curls and dressed carefully in stylish vintage Sunday best, Olive would settle her husband in a baggy suit and a hat which he would plant on his knee. The blood pressure checks and discussions around the common maladies of hard-working country folk led to a respectful rapport. As country folk often do, they made light of misfortune. An old tractor accident left Roger with a slight limp but his standard response to any comment was to slap his other leg and saying, 'This one's real good.'

Roger still managed to maintain a few nurseries around the original farmhouse on a road that bore the family name. Most of the valley had been cleared by his predecessors and some of the sons and daughters had married and settled locally.

They seemed to be aging gently in place with lots of loving help around; and so they were for a few years. I was called to see them only once, when Harry was having a brief 'funny turn', and, as I expected, the house was spick and span in a tidy garden. Slowly they wound the farm down. With age, life contracts to the size of a comfortable armchair which came, for them, with a view of a valley subdued and cultivated by generations.

The crunch came when Mrs Green almost apologetically mentioned a vague ache in some lower ribs that a previous doctor had dismissed. But there it was again. Local pressure produced pain, so I suggested a chest X-ray. The films weren't good. Lung cancer in a non-smoker that looked like secondary spread, most likely from old breast cancer, already disseminated to some ribs and, on further investigation, a few spots in the liver. These were not easy findings to present or digest but her questions were calm and focused. How long? What were the options and the odds? She was clear on having no chemotherapy or radiotherapy and left with quiet dignity after we discussed future palliative care and local community nursing support.

A week later Olive was back. After discussion with the children, she now wanted treatment. The oncologist and radiotherapist were consulted and when I saw her next, months later, she came alone, looking tired and wearing a helmet of curls now garishly synthetic. The cancer had spread further in the lungs and to other bones but Olive was more concerned about a new spot recently found in her brain. Olive wanted to know what symptoms she could she expect. How long would it take?

Again, not easy questions. She had only a little weight-loss, no significant cough or shortness of breath, no headaches or other signs of cerebral spread and as yet only mild bone pain easily controlled on low-dose painkillers, so I couldn't say her end was nigh but assured Olive of the close support available through her extended family and community nurses as her needs increased.

Somehow, against my protestations that there was as yet no real need, Olive persuaded me to see if a bed was available in 'that nice nursing home of yours' for a trial stay to 'see what it was like'; and, as it happened, a single room did come up right on the riverfront. The daughters helped her settle in. When the flowers were in the vases and they had ushered out the husband, I leant against the window sill with the river flowing past behind me as she finished composing herself in the bed.

'The bell is for room service and I'm just down the road if you need anything.'

'I just want to rest,' she sighed, pulling off the wig, which was tossed into a drawer that was then slammed shut. Olive slowly rubbed the few thin tufts of hair left on her scalp, then lay back in her pillows and lowered her eyelids. I was dismissed.

Olive slept well with the medication provided and a new ache in her mid-back settled quickly with only a slight increase in medication. The food 'wasn't up to scratch' – which is usually a good sign – but, despite visitors, Olive kept to her room with the wig off. The rounds of bus trips, concerts and other physical and communal activities organised for older people on a more gentle downward spiral were all politely declined. Olive ate in her room, the door closed, the thick curtains mostly drawn, in bed in a bed jacket with the blankets and coverlet smoothed around her.

After a week, the nurses told me Olive needed no assistance with toileting, showering or dressing. There had been no complaints of headache, nausea, visual disturbance, falls or confusion. There was, in fact, no reason for her to be there.

Again I leant against the windowsill with my back to the magnificent view. 'How are you feeling, Olive?' I opened.

'Well,' she said, 'I'm starting to have trouble with my crosswords and I don't want it to get worse and I don't want to go home and have my daughters fussing over me. So I'm ready to go now, if that's all right.'

'Ah, yes, well, um, there is, um, it is sometimes possible, in certain extreme circumstances …'

'What circumstances exactly?'

'Things like existential distress, unbearable reaction to impending death or poor symptom control.'

'Well, I think I qualify. What do I need to do?'

I spoke to the palliative care team in the local town. They suggested an antidepressant. I sent a concise letter detailing the case and, with Olive's grudging agreement, started an antidepressant. After a week I sent another letter to the experts advising the lack of benefit of the antidepressant (which hadn't really had time to have much effect) in a coherent woman with existential distress in whom terminal sedation seemed indicated.

This time a higher authority was invoked and indeed, the professor would visit in a few days if I could organise the family members to be present. They were.

Firstly, the professor asked Olive to explain her feelings, which she did very calmly, amid the tears and protestations of the daughters. Then the daughters were invited to speak, sob, sniffle and wail – which they did at length. Lastly, Roger was consulted. With misty eyes and trembling voice, he whispered, 'It's what Olive wants that matters.'

There was a pause before the professor summed up the appalling and hopeless prognosis Olive faced and went on to explain terminal sedation to the family. He appointed the doctor squatting in the corner to manage the process.

Olive was impatient for a quick and dignified exit but it took a few more days before we had all the nursing staff on-board. Religious qualms slowly crumbled in the face of, 'You wouldn't let your dog suffer like that would you?'

Olive woke only once after sedation was started.

'Am I still here?' she complained.

She was gone in three days.

MR WOODY

Forgive the levity but some sad tales need to be told lightly.

The doctor didn't meet Mr Williamson when he came into the dementia-specific, low-care facility. It was on his weekly visit a few days later that the nurse assigned to take him around the complex asked with a wry smile if he'd like to take on a new resident.

'Mrs Black has just gone to high care and, seeing you're so good with behaviours …' she said. In fact, as the newest doctor in town, he had no choice but to struggle with all the curly cases thrown at him; sudden arrivals catapulted by malign circumstance, dazed and kicking as they are bundled through a front door they'll never see again. Oh yes, he thought, he was great with 'behaviours'.

'OK, OK,' he groaned. 'What have you got?'

Robert Williamson had frontal dementia. It's a little like being a bit drunk. Punch-drunk. Frontal brain damage leads to a loss of critical judgement, a loss of decision-making skills and a loss of inhibitions. It seems this last characteristic was Robert's undoing.

On his first morning waking in a strange bed, he found himself with an erection. Unfortunately, the carer with whom he chose to share this wonder was less than enthusiastic, as the encounter was in a corridor and embellished with lavish flattery of her bust and other ramblings not entirely proper. Unfortunate because, rather than having a good laugh about it in the tea room, the carer in question had been deeply offended; and that seemed to set the tone for staff responses to Mr Williamson's ongoing exhibitionism and salaciousness, both excesses fitting neatly into the field of 'difficult behaviours'. Mr Williamson's wonderment at nature's morning glory continued but, in the midst of a harem of voluptuous handmaidens, he was confounded by their surliness and animosity towards his damning magnificence.

One of the carers was called in to report on events. She stood huge and outraged in the doorway, arms folded angrily over an ample bust. Something had to be done!

The doctor wrote a few notes as the door was closed and waited until the nurse was again seated before looking up. Then both he and the nurse cracked up. The nurse was on her second more manageable long-term relationship and no prude. She had also worked in disabilities prior to dementia, and Down syndrome boys often have an obsessive fascination with masturbation. Now there is a difficult behaviour to manage! What could the doctor say; what a to-do over an old man's stiffy!

Long ago, when the doctor was a young man and a nurse trainee in a large general hospital, he recalled a huge encounter with an enormous erection belonging to a young man who lay blithely in his bed with his hands behind his head as the nurse in question struggled to complete the pre-operative pubic shave. At that tender age, the doctor blushed easily and deeply. While changing the bowl of soapy water thick with tightly curled pubic hair for the third time in the pan room, he pleaded for advice from a senior nurse.

'Treat it like a gearstick!' she said sternly. 'First, second, reverse and you're done.'

Unfortunately, the doctor wasn't then a driver. At lunch that day in the staff dining room, the story caused great mirth. Several other nurses recalled similar situations amid emphatic plumes of cigarette smoke. Sadly, in today's age of possible elder abuse, 'whack it with a wooden spoon' no longer prompts the roars of laughter it did back then.

There are stories of drugs given to British sailors in the past to reduce sexual appetite, and hence the incidence of homosexuality, while confined together at sea. Today there are drugs to increase or decrease a man's tumescence. The doctor felt beholden to try something, so he ordered a drug which, on checking a text, was available for the reduction of drive in sexual deviations in men. It was immediately effective. Fortunately, Mr Williamson was way past noticing something no longer there. He seemed to settle in quite nicely.

On hearing about the case, an older colleague shared a story of using the same medication in the treatment of prostate cancer in an elderly priest. When explaining that the drug would also remove sexual desire the priest exclaimed with exasperation, 'Why couldn't they have given it to me when I was eighteen?'

If rashes or other problems occurred with Mr Williamson, the nurse thereafter recalled him as 'Mr Woody'. It was her little joke, which the doctor didn't encourage, but there you are, so to speak, life goes on. It was a few months before Mr Woody popped up again. It seems the tablets were losing their strength. A nurse had walked in on him *in flagrante* with another female resident. Showing great presence of mind, the nurse quietly withdrew. The next day Mr Williamson was complaining of a sore back and the lady concerned was a little sore 'down there'. Pain relief and emollients were considerately supplied, the doctors view in these cases was, 'Spare me the details and make sure there's lots of Sorbolene in the bathroom.' But sadly, this story didn't end there.

The family of the woman in question, who it seems was the one who had instigated the said congress, were less than amused with the nature of diversional therapy on offer. The following day she found herself unaccountably moved to another cottage where her husband could continue to visit infrequently and, while avoiding her blank stare, briefly hold her limp hand in his.

PHYLLIS

She came from another facility, a residential aged care facility, known as an RACF in the business, usually a hostel or nursing home; God's waiting rooms.

Her dementia was moderate. Still recognising family, still walking but only just, and with a lot of help. Prone to irritable outbursts, she was on two different tranquillisers and a nightly sedative. Her heels had shocking pressure sores that were both deep and foul-smelling.

Her children were angry. The staff tutted. The doctor arrived and tutted some more under the glaring eyes of family.

A few weeks later the family requested a meeting with the treating team. Phyllis had produced five children. Three lived in the city nearby. Two had married locally and stayed on the land. The husband and father was a nice old bloke but a certain amount of tension was palpable between the offspring. Some things can't be helped.

What they wanted was for the years to be rolled back and their mother of olden days returned to them. They wanted physiotherapists, public or privately engaged, to get Phyllis up and walking independently. They wanted her burgeoning weight controlled. Perhaps a dietician could be consulted? Could not the appropriate specialists reverse her decline in speech, vision and hearing? Their dear old Mum was failing. Surely it was the fault of the previous facility. Something had to be done, was the conclusion announced with baleful looks at the doctor.

The nurses and doctor smiled back gently. The heel ulcers were improving and, although Phyllis drowsed through a lot of the day, she did seem brighter. She was put on a new antidepressant and the tranquillisers had been reduced to only if needed – which they weren't. She slept fairly well at night without a sedative but was unable to get herself up to the toilet. She seemed to enjoy the group activities including exercise, news discussions, music and memory games. Her ears had been cleared, hearing-aid batteries changed and glasses adjusted, as were her dentures to a more comfortable fit of her shrinking jaw.

The doctor reduced her many medications as much as he could. Phyllis complained to the nurses about the large number of tablets the doctor was giving her. A pain-reducing skin patch had already proved effective in easing her back and hip pain. Changed weekly, the patch removed eight Panadol tablets a day (or fifty-six a week) from her 'medication burden'. Reluctantly agreeing to this, the city children had insisted on the continued treatment of mild hypertension and a near normal cholesterol level. It took a small bloodstained vomit to convince the family that even low-dose aspirin should be ceased.

Phyllis was no longer prone to anger or calling out at night. Her dexterity was slowly deteriorating and though described as a good eater, she was needing more assistance with meals. As time passed and her dementia progressed, Phyllis was unable to follow the exercise program. Her gait worsened slowly until even with a four-wheel walking frame she would need two staff to assist her on short walks.

With badly worn hips and knees, Phyllis was eventually confined to a large and deeply padded armchair on wheels and her bed. With good nursing care, her ulcers had healed. The children visited rarely. Her husband came every afternoon to sit with Phyllis for a while, only leaving after feeding her the evening meal.

Time passed. Months, then years went by. Though still smiling at the staff and the children when they appeared, her speech became increasingly minimal before ceasing altogether.

As her swallow became less well co-coordinated the spoon-fed mush would occasionally go down the wrong way and coughs would develop, known as aspiration pneumonia. With each episode the doctor would ring the eldest child and ask if antibiotics were desired. 'Of course!' was the reply. When oral antibiotics failed and the cough worsened, the children would insist on her transfer to hospital for intravenous antibiotics and assisted breathing. When the hospital returned her to the nursing home a week later the discharge summary would suggest an advanced care directive for comfort care in the nursing home be considered, rather than repeated admissions for recurrent pneumonia in an elderly nursing home patient with dementia.

'Oh no!' say the children on polite discussion with the doctor. 'Our mother deserves the best.'

A common consequence of aging began plaguing Phyllis: the fascia, or broad tendons of her hands, slowly contracted. The nurses applied pads as her fingers curled into fists. One of the children did some research and rang the doctor requesting surgical release of bilateral Dupuytren's contractures. The GP suggested Phyllis was a poor surgical candidate with a high risk of an adverse event including stroke, death or progression to advanced dementia, *severe* being a term out of fashion in this emotionally loaded area.

Nevertheless, the children prevailed and the GP wearily prepared a referral so that they could pay a higher authority to say no. When he discussed the proposed surgery with the husband the next day, the GP was pleased to discover the old gentleman was against any operations. After some honest discussion, the husband agreed to persuade his children to leave Phyllis in peace. It helped when an elderly nurse joined the discussion to gruffly comment that she certainly wouldn't put her mother through it.

When a further chest infection failed to respond to oral antibiotics, the children again insisted on transfer to hospital, where Phyllis was given two doses of intravenous antibiotics before being returned the next day with a further note suggesting that, in view of her advanced age and dementia, an advanced care directive was needed. It was touch and go for Phyllis but she slowly recovered. The local, country-raised children, used to dealing with sick and dying animals, understood the dilemma of active treatment versus comfort care for their mother, but the city kids stubbornly, indignantly refused to enter any discussion of future care or advanced care directives.

Time passed. The cough returned. The doctor did not bother to suggest comfort care but reflexively started oral antibiotics. Initially there was some improvement but the cough persisted. The doctor spoke with the husband. Should we keep her here and make her comfortable, the doctor asked gently. The husband understood; but on informing his children, again hospital transfer was requested. When the doctor described again the mute dementia, bed-and-chair-bound existence requiring feeding and changing, no longer aware of the children's existence, the eldest daughter agreed to discuss the situation with her siblings before getting back to him. She would try to visit the next day when the doctor emphasised her mother's precarious position.

There was no return phone call. As the cough took hold, Phyllis's breathing became rapid and laboured as she drifted in and out of consciousness. With her husband constantly by her side, she was prescribed small doses of morphine to slow the breathing, with another medication called midazolam to ease nausea and distress. Her heart stopped beating and she took her last breath at 3am, her husband still holding her hand in his.

The next day, as the doctor filled out the death certificate, the old nurse approached slowly with the rolling gait of worn hips, one hand held against her *nurses' back*.

'Ready for the next one, Doc?'

LOCAL WACKO

Archie was entering his final weeks when we met and was way too young to die. Older people can be philosophical but for people under sixty it's much scarier. An aging hippy and well-known local wacko, Archie lived alone with his animals in a remote bush humpy where two years ago he'd 'slipped in duck shit and broke my neck'. It turned out to be a pathological fracture due to secondary cancer from an undiagnosed primary in his prostate. In his own words, 'Basically, I'm fucked.'

It was hard to disagree. For two years Archie told all his friends and many acquaintances in the area that when the time came, he would take himself out. His elderly mother who lived in Melbourne would come and stay each year in the nearby town so she could visit her son, who had migrated south twenty years earlier with a hippy influx when the local apple market was lost and small farms were sold off cheaply. The town still sports rainbow signs, an eastern import clothes shop and has an annual folk festival. Archie had been a talented musician who played in various local bands and was also sought after for his stone-wall work which, in hilly riverside land, was very popular.

Slowly the cancer spread through his skeleton and Archie began to lose weight. A fall from a chair while evoking his flamboyant past as a guitarist led to a crush fracture in his spine and the onset of chronic pain. Fear of pain led to rapid escalation of dosages. Love of procrastination led to perpetual delaying of the time to take his life until further falls and fractures made it unsafe for him to live alone. Friends came over, took all his guns and threw them in the river, or so the story goes. After a failed overdose of sequestered painkillers, he was too weak to manage alone and unwillingly moved in with his mother in town. Calling on all his contacts, Archie again collected a lot of medication which he washed down with alcohol. When he woke two days later, he cursed his mother, who had sat and watched his hardly breathing body; all that time caught in an agony of indecision, to help her son's wish or call an ambulance. After further falls, probably some brain damage and increasing pain, he was eventually admitted to the palliative care unit attached to the main hospital in the city for terminal care and – as Archie understood it, and as his mother and friend assured me was true – for terminal sedation.

After some weeks in the unit, his use of physical painkillers had been weaned while strong steroids quickly reduced the deep boring pain of the swelling within bones. The pronounced side effects of steroids are mood elevation, increased appetite and loquaciousness. Psychological agents were introduced to reduce distress. Archie continued to demand an end to his suffering but then would want just a bit more time to write something else important that had to be recorded in his diary. A phone call was made. Would a local nursing home accept care of a young man dying of metastatic prostate cancer who had been admitted for terminal care but then stabilised and was unsafe for discharge to home.

A deathly thin fifty-five-year-old turned up in a wheelchair with an urbane mother, demanding the terminal sedation he'd been promised but refused in the big hospital. Talking now exhausted him, he spoke in whispered expletives. I promised to get to the bottom of his story but in the meantime needed to write up his current medication cocktail to keep things on an even keel, and made sure he was aware of the availability of 'as required' medication for pain, which of course he was. His mother meekly followed me outside the room to quietly reinforce her son's conviction that his further decline was unnecessary and he had been promised terminal sedation. It's not a term one expects to hear slip from the lips of a well-coiffured eighty-year-old but, despite her religious convictions otherwise, she was now her son's advocate with greater conviction and needed me to know that.

The registrar from the hospital was quite helpful. Terminal sedation had been discussed but Archie's repeated delays in setting a time frame and then the medication changes which stabilised his condition meant that his fear and anguish became an unsolvable dilemma – unsolvable and, inevitably, as the registrar pointed out, irrelevant in the face of impending death. All very well for you, I thought, and asked a few nurses who tended to be local if they knew of Archie. Slowly the story above unfolded. Everyone had an Archie story. How he'd often leave an evening with people only to playfully reappear with a further final comment. Again and again, he was known for it. The local vet was horrified when she realised the man who had asked her for some of 'whatever she uses on animals to put them down' was still alive. An older friend of the mother had bought in his dogs and cat to be euthanised as soon as Archie had gone to town, saying he was dying then. No wonder he declined home visits. Some friends had managed to organise the care of one dog before the older woman took control. How much was this tragedy responsible for his ongoing misery?

Soon mostly bed bound, Archie would say he was comfortable, able to eat and drink small amounts but that his life was intolerable and he wanted it ended now. The team was called and a registrar and social worker duly arrived and heard Archie's repeated plea and his mother's apologetic support. Archie clearly fitted the criteria surrounding the use of terminal sedation in exceptional circumstances and written approval was virtually promised. In a subsequent debrief with the registrar, social worker and nurses, the registrar asked me if I'd been involved in any other cases like this. Only one, I lied, in someone much older.

Archie's mood didn't improve. 'They'll never let me,' he cursed in whispers; but with prodding, a letter did arrive a week later granting formal approval and, after one last day's procrastination, the process was begun. So close to death already, it only took a nudge. In a day Archie was gone.

MATILDA

No-one was home. Mute in all the current nurses' collective memory, never visited, immobile, no past, no future, only a name, Matilda.

So old, she had outlived her doctor. Another was sought. He was not so young but eager to please and smooth the way where he could. What are all these pills for? he questioned the nurses rhetorically. Pills for high blood pressure, pills for high cholesterol, pills for bone density and blood-thinning and mood elevation, pills to keep the spoonfuls of pureed food moving though the inert silent receptacle that was called Matilda.

'Ha!' cried the doctor as he slashed most of the dastardly drugs from the medication chart and strode away.

A week later the nurses called him back. Tears of some unreadable tragedy slowly coursed down Matilda's time-ravaged cheeks. The doctor and nurses shuddered in the presence of such unbearable anguish. The antidepressant was hastily recommenced and soon the tears stopped. A smidgin of brashness was knocked off the not so young doctor.

VERA'S END

Vera was a true salt of the earth type: old and wiry, of hard-working country stock; widowed for many years and adored by children and grandchildren. I always savoured her dry, self-deprecating humour. Vera still got about and even enjoyed the occasional drink at the local. The town had been shocked five years earlier when Vera took up with a knockabout bloke of similar vintage. Her disapproving daughter confided that he would never last and, indeed, Vera and Tom had occasional disagreements that led to Tom disappearing for a few days or even a week at a time. But then they would reappear together, Tom the attentive partner and Vera beaming ear to ear.

I examined Vera a few times when, grudgingly, she let Tom drag her in with a bad cough or a swollen knee. At Vera's age there wasn't much flesh left on her frame but she was generally feisty and uncomplaining. The daughter's indignation was somewhat subdued by an appreciation of the mutual courtesies displayed by these two old folks who could still find comfort in each other's arms in the cold nights. Vera's sundry aches and rashes were easy to fix but I let them all know the obvious in various half-serious ways. It was Vera's failing heart that was the real issue. She was living on borrowed time. Bigger drugs were introduced to buy a bit more.

As her weakness progressed, I started visiting their humble home whenever Tom rang with some new medical drama. Eventually it became clear Vera's heart was finally giving out. Initially Vera tried to hide the magnitude of her symptoms for fear of being sent to hospital, but the seriousness of her condition became plain to Tom. In the kitchen, a red-faced son insisted it was illegal to die at home and that his mother would have to go to hospital, but Vera was keen to stay put in her cosy council flat and with Tom devotedly at her side, so it was agreed to let her stay and keep her comfortable. The extended family was called together to break the news that was news to no-one.

One of the many grandchildren had some nursing experience and the family rostered themselves for continuing care and support. Now daily visiting was often more involved with calming various family members huddling outside smoking on the front porch than dealing with Vera herself, who was drifting in and out of consciousness as her kidneys shut down in the final days. The last morning that I visited, early before work, sensing the end was nigh, I was confronted by a distraught Tom pacing outside chain-smoking.

'Doc, Doc,' he muttered, 'tell me I'm not mad.'

He had been sitting in the bedroom all night listening to Vera's slowing breathing when a middle-aged man appeared in the room and bent over Vera's unconscious form for some time.

'Doc, I knew him from the photos. He was the dead husband.'

I reassured Tom as best I could that dead relatives often appear around the time of death. Vera never regained consciousness and died later that day.

THE PLATEAU

He wanted a new doctor. He lived precariously on a plateau between life and death. Sometimes people hover there with no hope of recovery, the odds against them, but somehow the downward trajectory of their lives is temporarily halted and, in spite of imminent demise, they 'plateau' for days to months before resuming the descent to inevitable death. He had lingered for years, bed-bound, needing constant nursing care, intermittent oxygen, morphine and other medications to maintain his failing body, his obedient wife by his side every day massaging his feet, wheeling him out into the sun, setting up the video player, discreetly wiping the saliva from the side of his mouth as he talked to me in a thick German accent.

He wanted antibiotics for a chronic cough. He was over ninety, semi-paralysed, heart failing, lung cancer never fully cleared, and having trouble clearing his throat. Antibiotics weren't really indicated but he had asked for another doctor and antibiotics he would have with the judicious addition of a mucolytic (to clear mucous) and a few other minor adjustments to ease his difficulties.

The cough seemed to ease. Other changes made him a little more comfortable. He talked of being a soldier in the Second World War. The doctor had to reassure him that the current nurses involved in his care carried no resentment or knowledge of his involvement as the *enemy*, that he was not *persona non grata*, that the nurses cared for everyone without prejudice whether their needs were minor or time-consuming like his. Then came the questions regarding his prognosis. He thought the lung cancer had been cleared. Caught out, the doctor clumsily explained it had not. The response was stoic. The doctor belatedly promised all efforts would be made to maintain his comfort and dignity as restrictions on morphine and sedatives were relaxed.

A week later the nurses called. Things had taken a grave turn. The doctor arrived just as he breathed his last breath, his wife heaving sobs of grief and relief.

YOU MAY NOT FIND THIS AMUSING

But I have to. I was working a Saturday morning GP shift: nothing booked, everything an emergency, but with an experienced receptionist and nurse on board to field things, it wasn't a bad morning, or so I thought. Four days later the clinic manager stepped into my office at the end of the day to ask if I'd been having a bad day last Saturday, as there had been a complaint, and did I remember a patient called Blair?

It had been a busy morning; the name meant nothing to me but on opening his record the encounter came back vividly. An impossible three-year-old climbing the walls and a mother sitting with a long story full of complaint about the treatments and progress so far for her dear Blair, who was running rampant, turning the taps on and off and jumping on and off the scales despite her ineffectual entreaties. After five minutes of deciphering the mother's complex account of events leading to the visit, I was tiring of the child's hyperactivity and the mother's ineffectual parenting skills. I'm afraid I told Blair to sit in his chair and be still in a rather stern and slightly raised voice. It worked. As the story of his woes was winding up, he started wiggling to get up but then froze again with a sudden pointed finger and a sharp word. The examination was quick, the treatment swiftly delivered and off they went.

Was I having a bad day? No. but it was a Saturday. I just didn't have the time to gain the child's trust, to open my drawer of toys and diversions, spinning coloured lights and a small sound-effects board that laughs or applauses or farts or many other things at the press of a button. Children love it, patents hate it but it all takes time, and the stern doctor approach was fast and effective.

The manager was conciliatory. She understood the rising tide of little darlings but the mother's phone call complained about the cold doctor's traumatisation of dear little Blair. My response was indignation at this incompetent mother's indignation. I professed to be more than happy to defend my decision-making and child-management skills in any further complaint forum.

Then I went home and recounted the tale to my partner, who was appropriately despairing of modern parenting styles and the brazen audacity to complain; which helped for about five minutes until I remembered that my old professional partner – a father of three highly successful adults, and a GP particularly skilled with children – would have taken the time to charm or admonish dear blameless Blair more gently and the encounter would have resolved without offence.

I rang the Mother the next day to apologise for my poor child-management skills and my call was appreciated. She would take the matter no further. I thanked her without choking. A complaint, whether cleared or not, would follow my career for life.

But in terms of what is acceptable GP demeanour, and what is not, I remember a story I was once told.

What I didn't add was that quite a long time ago my great grandfather had a large parlour in a small town which was used once a week by an elderly GP who travelled by horse and trap over a mountain pass from the larger town where his practice was based.

Some years ago, I went to a family gathering in the town organised by a cousin and oral historian. I travelled from the city with my father and an old woman who also grew up in the same town, and she told us the following story which caused great mirth.

When she was about five years old, she remembered her mother taking her to see the elderly doctor because her mother thought she was tongue-tied and that her frenulum, the skin that tethers the tongue to base of the mouth, needed to be snipped a little.

'Don't be ridiculous!' roared the doctor. 'No woman is tongue-tied. Take her away!'

'And to this day,' said the old lady, 'I still have trouble with my S's when I get excited.'

THE SCALLYWAG

Ralph was a hulking giant of a man. An ex-boxer, his voice was deep and loud. Gruff greetings to the receptionists of the medical clinic would boom around the waiting room and reverberate down a corridor of consulting rooms through to the tea room at the rear of the building, where heads would tilt and nod with murmurs of his name.

A seventy-five-year-old paranoid schizophrenic, Ralph saw his GP for monthly long-acting antipsychotic injections. A veteran of various abdominal surgeries for bowel cancer, Ralph also saw an oncologist for weekly chemotherapy at the local hospital. He was a long-term survivor.

Over time Ralph came to trust the new doctor at the clinic, a doctor who himself had known more schizophrenics than most, including a close friend from childhood.

Of all the different forms of mental aberration, schizophrenia seems the maddest. Mad as fruit cakes, mad as meat axes, mad as cut snakes. They say neurotics build castles in the air and psychotics live in them. Good luck to them, the doctor thought. Sanity seemed cursed by dullness, whereas madness brought a breath of fresh air into the office with flights of fancy and fits of inspiration to mitigate the ever-present risk of impending chaos.

Many years ago, as a young trainee nurse, the doctor had spent time in a psychiatric hospital. Middle-class, middle-aged women having a come-apart were one thing, but the true nutters he found a bit scary. Encouraged to engage with the in-patients, he listened to a woman complaining that her washing machine talked to her. Slightly amused, he asked her what it said.

'YOU DON'T OWN ME!' She spat back.

There are different categories of schizophrenia, paranoid being the most common. Sunglasses are never lost, they are stolen. Voices, always malicious, emanate from light fittings and power points. Car stickers carry personal mystic meanings, everything is synchronistic. Radio and TV are filled with secret messages. Malign omens are everywhere. Tablets and injections help to dull the intensity but often also deaden the so-called positive symptoms – inspiration and increased creativity – more than the negative symptoms of depression, apathy and the evil intent of the voices and messages.

Not surprisingly, few schizophrenics stay on treatment. If they have repeated bizarre behaviours that conflict with others and bring them repeatedly before the law, then community treatment orders are made and compulsory antipsychotic injections, weekly or monthly, are administered by hardened teams of community psychiatric nurses with varying degrees of success. Or they see a GP.

Sometimes, perversely, physical illness seems to make mental illness abate. The voices may quieten as the cancer spreads. It was the best that could be hoped for Ralph. His voices got worse at night; less distraction. Sometimes they kept him awake. He was on tablets in the evening which he took because they helped a little. Then again, he was convinced his voices were real. The doctor didn't argue. The monthly needles were the fault of the government, part of a larger conspiracy, Ralph kindly reassured the doctor.

Perhaps the bowel cancer did help to lessen the severity of his madness. The weekly chemotherapy didn't seem to. He was always weak and nauseous for a few days afterwards. Sometimes he would ring complaining of the side effects. The doctor would visit and, depending on the severity of the vomiting or diarrhoea, would decide if Ralph needed to go back into hospital. His sisters would also ring the GP if they were concerned about Ralph, who was often determinedly nonchalant.

'Don't send me back there, Doc!'

His oncologist was known to continue treatment longer than most. When Ralph asked his GP whether he should persist, the doctor found it hard to tread a delicate line between advice and influence.

'Well, Ralph, what do you think? Is it worth it?'

The doctor would go up to the 'big house' to see how Ralph was recovering from each further bout of overwhelming side effects. After a week or two of intravenous fluids, good nursing care and a break from the chemotherapy, Ralph would slowly improve and return home, only to recommence the weekly infusions of cytotoxic therapy.

As the years passed, Ralph and the doctor fell into a comfortable friendship. They generally went to lunch once a week so the doctor could keep an eye on him. It was time-consuming to debrief the man, to ask the right questions, check his legs to monitor the level and degree of swelling, listen to the latest complaints, adjust the many medications, trial something else to help any new issues and try to keep an even keel. Then came the interpretation of specialist opinions, test results and treatment reviews.

Picking Ralph up for lunch once a week gave the doctor a mutually pleasant way to complete the process, often in the drive to and from lunch while enjoying a jolly respite from food often grabbed on the job or consumed while driving between nursing homes.

With gentle prodding over these lunches the snippets of Ralph's life formed a larger portrait. Always a bit of a lad, he had hit the streets in adolescence and taken up residence in disused garage in Sydney. Eventually he met a girl. They married and had four children. Then he lost all five in a car accident returning from a holiday. Ralph was spared by his absence due to an affair. Not surprisingly, the voices in his head started with the subsequent guilt and grief.

The GP preferred home visits rather than sitting behind a desk. The habit of weekly lunches became comfortably entrenched. A former taxi driver, Ralph knew all the backstreet shortcuts of the area. They laughed a lot together. Sometimes Ralph would suddenly stop talking and look around the cafe with wide eyes and plead, 'I'm not talking to loud, am I?'

'No, Ralph. No.'

It quickly became apparent which cafe proprietors had some appreciation of mental illness. Perhaps they had an afflicted relative or some other experience which told them that Ralph was someone a bit special.

Fairly early in the friendship, the sister living closest to Ralph suggested the doctor join her and her husband with Ralph at a bowling club for dinner one night – to get his measure, the doctor supposed. Why had he befriended the old man? Aware of the unspoken question, the doctor was cordial but vague about personal details. Truth was, Ralph was a jolly old soul who melted hearts. On this evening he was simply pleased to have everyone together outside of the doctor's usual professional constraints so that they could all enjoy a beer or two. The food was awful, but with Ralph they all praised it.

The doctor was interstate when Ralph's last admission to hospital arrived. He felt at a loss when he returned from a break with aging parents to find Ralph gone, departed, dead. There had been no phone calls, no texts. The family knew the doctor was away.

'Don't bother the Doc,' Ralph would have said, always apologetic for ringing when he was poorly.

At the wake the doctor saw for the first time photos of Ralph, the young larrikin and then the married man. It was wonderful to see him young and happy. The Ralph he had known was old and haunted by his madness. The doctor didn't linger despite the pleas of the sisters to stay. The family were very appreciative but the doctor felt his presence was putting a damper on a family deep in grief.

About a month after the death the doctor had a dream that didn't fade away on waking, as dreams do, but stayed vivid in his memory. Ralph had come back. He gave the doctor a bear hug like long lost friends. They spent a carefree summer's day together; fishing, swimming, eating and laughing. Life was a holiday without doctors or diseases or deadlines. Ralph seemed to be apologising for leaving so suddenly without saying goodbye.

At the end of the day they lay down together and slept on a grassy bank somewhere, in the dream, in each other's arms. They spooned.

When the doctor awoke Ralph was gone but the feeling stayed. The dream left a strong sense of love and thanks that had never been acknowledged while Ralph was alive. The doctor had always been careful not to mention his own same-sex partner. Sexuality was a complication best avoided. With paranoid schizophrenia, trust is a fragile thing.

Ralph drank at the local bowling club and over the last summer the doctor had taken up bowls with a few friends – a local nurse who worked with the doctor in a nursing home and her partner, both keen bowlers and members of the same club – and his partner. Ralph and the doctor would enjoy a cold one while watching and chatting with other players.

Getting a bit beery as the light faded, the doctor would be introduced to a colourful array of Ralph's drinking partners in the clubhouse who all had a soft spot for the charming old codger. The nursing friend had an innate sense of how to get on with Ralph and after the bowling green they would all sit together and have a merry time made more precious by a sense of impermanence and impending doom.

The doctor ran into one of Ralph's sisters, months after the wake, and told her he'd been visited by Ralph in a dream to say goodbye and be given a hug. They both teared up, across the counter between them.

'Me too,' she said.

THE OLD DOG

'Look,' the GP, feeling jaded, was saying to the case manager. 'He's got moderate dementia. He won't manage at home. His son won't take him on. We can't fix his chronic anaemia. When do we stop the transfusions? What's the point of prolonging his life if he's bound for a nursing home?'

Bill was a nice old ninety-two-year-old who had recovered well after a fall in the garden and a fractured shoulder, but he was increasingly frail and now deemed a high falls risk. For over a month since his discharge from the hospital he had been in a transitional care unit for what's known as slow rehabilitation. The unit functions primarily as a dumping ground for the hospital, enabling fast discharges of predominantly elderly guests who have undergone some calamity and been patched up, so to speak, but were still unsafe to send home. A TCU admission gives a dedicated team of doctors, nurses, physiotherapists and occupational therapists time to see what improvements can be made in strength and independence. Will some time for feeding-up and further recovery with gentle physiotherapy allow discharge for home alone? Home visits are organised pre-discharge. Occupational therapists tut-tut over any loose rugs or extension cords while new ramps or rails are arranged. Can they make a hot drink, get out of their armchair easily and use the bathroom independently? Additional supports are garnered, either from family and/or community services with follow-up visits to monitor progress.

If deemed unsafe for discharge to home, then the options are retirement village, hostel or nursing home. Sometimes, when patients or family disagree with the considered suggestion of 'assisted living', the unit is forced to send them home to fail, and hope the consequences aren't fatal.

In this case, the team had done their best but Bill was still needing a lot of nursing assistance and had failed his home visit. He was too weak, and this was complicated by his anaemia, a decreased ability of his blood to carry oxygen. Multiple investigations had revealed no active bleeding, yet his haemoglobin (a marker for this condition) kept dropping, contributing to his lethargy and requiring more frequent blood transfusions to restore him.

The doctor waved the last blood test to emphasise the dilemma. Bill's haemoglobin was again 'in his boots'. It was a Friday and the team had planned to send him home on Monday. He was resisting transfer to a nursing home and his son, although caring, lived in a nearby city with a young family and was not prepared to take him in.

Once the trial discharge had failed, a nursing home placement seemed inevitable.

The case manager looked up at the doctor. 'Well, yes,' she said slowly, 'but what about his dog?' Knowing just when to pull the heart strings. As the doctor paused, she added, 'Doesn't he deserve just one more chance?'

'Oh, all right,' the doctor said, 'I'll go and have a chat with him.'

'Please, Doc,' Bill said from his bed, 'Me dog's off his tucker, he's hardly eaten since I've been away. The neighbours tried everything.'

'OK, all right,' the GP said with a sigh, 'I'll talk to the hospital', knowing that the emergency department specialist would plead no beds and a hopeless case. Bill's presumed slow intestinal bleed had never been found on scopes and so was untreatable; besides which, any surgery would be contraindicated in a man of his age with his co-morbidities: a 'dicky heart' and dementia which could easily progress irreversibly after a general anaesthetic.

When the doctor rang 'the big house' the response was as he anticipated. Is there an advanced care plan?

Has he been asked the big questions?

'Yes, yes,' he said, 'conservative treatment, no life-prolonging measures.'

There was a long pause.

'But look, he's a nice old codger,' the GP pleaded over the phone. 'He's worried about his old dog. Could you just top him up one more time and send him back so we can get him home for one last try on Monday?

'Oh, all right,' came the weary reply. 'Send him up!'

SPARE US FROM THE WELL-MEANING

THE CALL CAME on a Saturday night in the middle of a social evening and after a few gins but the nurse sounded stressed. Two brothers were insisting on a doctor's attendance in a nursing home after being informed their mother, Agnes, seemed to have taken a turn for the worse after recently returning from hospital with a new diagnosis of cancer. Fair enough, but the nurse warned of discord between the brothers about treatment and pleaded with me to come soon.

On arrival I quickly read the notes from the hospital before meeting the waiting sons. It seemed that two weeks ago black stools and abdominal pain had prompted an emergency transfer to the local hospital where a diagnosis of renal cancer was made from various tests, including scans showing an intra-abdominal mass of considerable size. The presence of the cancer was not a surprise, as a visit to the hospital seven months earlier after a fall had prompted an incidental note of evidence pointing to renal cancer; but considering her advanced age, then almost ninety, and her severe dementia and heart failure, treatment with no hope of cure was discussed with the two sons and declined. Agnes had returned, this time only a few days earlier, but as I was on holiday and Agnes had been stable, I was not aware of her return to the nursing home, where her husband Raymond visited daily from the adjacent hostel. The nurse had recognised the onset of a glazed look and rapid breathing as signs of imminent demise, hence the call.

A quick look at the patient confirmed the nurse's intuition. The patient was indeed moribund, drifting in and out of consciousness, rouse-able but unable to swallow, breathing fast and shallowly, her husband sitting beside her holding her hand helplessly. Packing away his tools of trade, the doctor gathered the sons and husband for a frank chat in another room.

'I'm sorry, but I would agree with the nurse. Your mother is passing away and, from the information sent back with her the hospital, it is clear there is no hope of cure. There is nothing more we can do now apart from keep her comfortable.'

It wasn't quite as blunt as that but the husband began to sob quietly and the sons jumped to each side of him supportively. The son who had demanded a doctor's presence also wanted to know why transfer back to hospital wasn't appropriate at this point. It was gently explained that Agnes would have better care here with nurses who knew her well and with her husband at her side. Suggesting some medication to help slow her breathing and make her more comfortable provoked a loud outburst from one of the sons and accusations of medical indifference to the elderly and a conspiracy of doing away with them. The doctor explained that if it was his mother, he would want her to be more comfortable; but as Agnes was past complaining of discomfort, the doctor compromised by leaving written orders for something to be given to relieve discomfort if distress became more obvious overnight and the brothers could agree that something given to ease this was appropriate.

On Monday things were much the same. Swelling had moved from one arm to the other as the mass pressed on various blood vessels, and I had to order that her rings be cut off to prevent occlusive pain. But still she lingered on the edge of death for another three days.

When I arrived to confirm the death and complete the death and cremation forms, the more rational of the sons was leaving. He shook my hand, thanked me for 'dropping in' and explained that his mother had just passed away as he had wanted, after an injection.

The same registered nurse was in the office where I went to complete the paperwork after viewing the body. She told me how she had pleaded with the sons to let her give morphine to Agnes for days after I had had been called in, as the strain of continued gasping was showing more clearly in her tired and frightened old face. Reluctantly, the family agreed after reassurance that it was unlikely to kill her. The morphine dose was a low, test dose and did little to relieve the gasping and soon wore off. Again, the nurses pleaded but the sons argued for their mother's right to die naturally, without undue medical interference. They were Christians, they explained carefully, and didn't believe in assisted death or any treatment that may accelerate death, refusing to accept the concept of dose titration. The day before Agnes died, two registered nurses asked, together, if she would like something to ease her breathing and she, in one of those rare lucid moments the demented can display, said clearly that she needed medical help.

Still, the Christian sons were against further interventions that may accelerate death – not understanding that a little is not necessarily a lot – so their mother gasped on for six days with only a few short-acting injections in that time, the last a full two-and-a half hours before her death. Now if morphine had caused her death, it would have been twenty minutes after administration when the blood level reached a maximum and before it began to wane – but really, what was the point of arguing with these ignorant, prejudiced and downright rude 'Christians'?

What most annoyed me was that the anguished death of Agnes could have been so easily mitigated, that her level of dementia was unlikely to yield any great insights into her life or those around her, as is often the case in conscious dying, where morphine is only used intermittently or not at all for spasms of pain. Agnes was way past meaningful last words and her last gasping six days on this earth could have been so easily smoothed without undue shortening of life with the right titration or dose adjustment according to response, starting slow and working up to the desired effect of simply relieving suffering.

The nurses felt their duty of care was blocked by relatives who were rude and not deferential to the long-term, lowly paid and overworked carers of their mother. If I had known – if I was not on holiday at the time, moving house – and not kept fully cognisant of the progress of events by nurses also caring for *me*, I might have been able to convene another meeting with the sons and exhorted them again to reconsider the manner of their mother's passing. Perhaps this story will help others. Perhaps the sons' deaths will be as long and anguished as the one they provided their dear mother.

LOU: A SAD TALE OF SLOW DEATH AND A LAST SMILE

Lou came into the nursing home under another doctor, who didn't visit often, so the family asked around and I got a call, would I see her? Her time was near. Cancer had spread through one lung and into the lining of her abdominal organs. At eighty-six, she looked emaciated with an obscenely enlarged abdomen, breathing a little hard on oxygen but uncomplaining, resigned to her fate.

The original diagnosis was made four years earlier. Then living alone in a fibro cottage that she and her husband had moved into thirty-five years earlier, on a waterfront now surrounded by McMansions, Lou decided against active treatment. The use of oxygen for bouts of shortness of breath had become continuous before increasing frailty and falls catapulted Lou into hospital and eventual nursing home placement. Her husband was long dead and the children were either far away or had their hands full, but still visited.

Lou announced on arrival that she had had enough but two months passed – as her stomach slowly swelled and her appetite failed – before we met. On one lung, Lou was not short of breath while on oxygen, but was soon gasping if the oxygen was turned off for any reason. Even so, Lou was more bothered by the recent mental clouding caused by a new sedating antidepressant, added to aid sleep on top of a regular sleeping tablet and a twice-daily medication to relieve anxiety, both of which were added after her last fall, which recently led to a few days in the local hospital.

On top of this was increasing difficulty swallowing all her tablets, including many for the pointless treatment of blood pressure, high cholesterol and osteoporosis. With poor gastric absorption complicated by nausea, Lou was pleased to have all her tablets ceased and medication given subcutaneously to control her pain, respiratory rate, air hunger, nausea and anxiety. Lou thanked me for her cleared thinking. She could talk sensibly with her family and friends.

Then there was a new fear of confinement, of claustrophobia. Advancing weakness, weight loss and another fall rendered her bed-bound. Lou was moved to the palliative care room, where the door and blinds were kept open. It was a larger room, furnished less like a nursing home, with pictures on the wall: coastal horizons and a print of Jesus, one of those sweet young man versions with a full head of curly hair, flowing beard and beatific smile beaming down from a cheap frame while Lou laboured on below with her one lung and increasingly distended abdomen.

Even so, with the changes and a room with a view, Lou entered a certain plateau: a period of apparent stabilisation or even improvement often seen before the final decline towards death. Only minor adjustments were needed to maintain the impasse, the indefinite stalemate between life and death.

On reviewing doses one morning, Lou confided to me that sleep was her favourite time and that she would like to sleep all the time, as she only felt happy for a few minutes after waking. I said that if she stayed asleep more it might bring her death sooner rather than later, to which she replied, 'I don't mind, my children know what I want.'

Now there happens to be a subclause in a law somewhere that allows a doctor to relieve the suffering of existential distress in a hopeless situation using terminal sedation. Not the sort of thing to do without a specialist authorisation, so I rang the local palliative care service and was eventually put through to the roving community specialist on his hands-free car phone. Fortunately, he had time, but unfortunately, no sympathy for my call. He refused to see the patient or consider the request as anything but euthanasia.

I thanked him for his opinion and asked if he would mind if I discussed the case with any of his colleagues, which he did not baulk at, although he added that they would likely all agree with him.

EVIL CONJECTURES

The only other specialist doctor from the team available that day was doing a round at the local hospital but was kind enough to take my call. She was similarly unimpressed with such a grey area of law and would not countenance supporting the proposed treatment with no convincing loss of symptom control that could be urgently and expertly managed. Again, I was as polite as possible, thanking her for her extended but fruitless opinion. And then – surprise, surprise – five minutes later she rang back offering to discuss the case with her colleagues, the remaining two of whom were unavailable until Monday and one of them would visit by Wednesday. At last, I thought, someone else will hear this tragic tale.

Alack, alas, the addition of knockout drops to promote sleep was a bonus, but the opinion was not favourable. Lou enjoyed her food, it seemed. Well, yes, until she ate more than a little, and then would feel nauseous for hours. She enjoyed crosswords. Well, yes, but it had been weeks since she was able to sit up and use a pen. She was mostly comfortable. Well, yes, with constant oxygen and morphine. She was not actively dying yet. Well, no – that was the point.

We did our best to keep her comfortable. Lou continued to ask various staff to deliver a knockout dose but I had to admit to her that my hands were tied. The last palliative car specialist had made it clear that if I chose to ease Lou's suffering and hasten her end, and if a nurse then made a compliant and the case went to court, my position would be officially indefensible. Not the sort of back-up I was hoping for.

With a sense of helplessness in the face of hopelessness, I visited Lou most days to sit and monitor and make minor changes to ease the bouts of oxygen hunger and anxiety and help her sleep through the long nights. We moved her back into a shared room with three other women for company. As the gauntness of her features slowly increased, the lingering face-off between life and death dragged on for another twenty-four days before an infection took hold in her remaining lung. Would we let a dying dog lie gasping so long? In her last lucid moment with me, while holding my hand and smiling up at me, she said to her ever present son,

'I love this doctor.'

Which I thought was much undeserved, but it did help me feel a little less useless.

Lou was moved back to the single room. Further increases in morphine doses to ease the more rapid breathing may or may not have brought forward her death; but if so, not by much. Lou finally succumbed to her fate four days later, alone, hopefully in her sleep, in the early hours of the morning.

A SNIPPET OF A STORY ...

THIS STORY is not about death. I include it as a portrait of my mother. A true story, I was the third child mentioned.

The kitchen was warm with the smell of baking scones but still her mind could not settle. The cream was whipped and the strawberry jam she had made herself sat in matching cut-glass bowls at either end of a freshly pressed tablecloth bordered with garlands of flowers perfectly embroidered by her own hand. The best china sat waiting around a small vase holding fresh roses from the garden. When the doorbell rang Mary had just enough time to pour milk into a jug and put the bottle back in the fridge before taking her apron off and patting her hair as she moved to open the front door.

Within fifteen minutes five women had arrived to fill the kitchenette with squeals of laughter as babies were handed about and balanced on knees and a few toddlers played together in a wooden child pen on the floor. A cat weaved through the high heels and nappy smells with its tail held high in disdain.

The level of hilarity belied the simple tea they quaffed, yet this was long before gin and tonics and talk of teenage pregnancy. This was a time of cracked nipples and mastitis, of nasty nappy rashes and squints and, although salves and cold cabbage leaves were bandied about, the hostess felt brittle and unable to talk about her own distress as she poured more tea. Her third baby was flawed, she increasingly feared – no, was convinced – just as his two elder brothers had been before the local doctor intervened. Twice she had seen him snip the skin with surgical scissors still warm from the steaming sterilizer. Twice she had held her babies tightly, rocking them as the screams subsided.

Tongue-tied, the words caused her to shiver.

'What is it, Mary?' one of the women suddenly shot at her. 'What's on your mind? Something is bothering you.'

'Oh, June,' she said, 'nothing really, but I think Arthur is a bit tongue-tied and I know if I take him to the doctor, I'll have to talk him into it. It's not as bad as the first two kids had it – but still.' Relieved to be sharing her worry at last, she went on. 'Geoffrey doesn't think it matters but I think diction is so important; I don't want him sounding like a country bumpkin.'

The women murmured their sympathy and someone complained of a brother with webbed feet; but still, Mary felt unconsoled. A country girl who'd married a city bloke, she looked out across the town to the harbour as the women chattered on. She wanted only perfect children in a perfect world but where was the time to argue with the doctor? There was the late summer fruit to bottle, the garden to weed and prune, the house to maintain spotlessly without a hint of effort or complaint before her husband returned from work, the children bathed, the dinner on and perhaps a dab of perfume.

As a young lass she had watched her older brothers gut and hang carcasses in the shed as she changed the meat-laden liquid in the hanging glass fly traps as quickly as she could. She had held sheep steady as thick elastic bands were applied to the base of their scrotums; she was a farmer's daughter and then a mother craft nurse before her marriage.

When all the women in their bright dresses had left and the table was cleared, when the tablecloth was soaking and the washing-up all done, dried and put away, Mary popped a pot of water on to boil and into it she slipped a pair of her sharpest stainless steel sewing scissors.

ACKNOWLEDGEMENTS

Lindsay Allen, encouragement and financial assistance.

Danny Blackman, encouragement and financial assistance.

Robyn Bowles, editorial assistance and support.

Leigh Edwards, editorial and technical assistance.

Robert Edwards, proofing, support.

Sarah Elliss, support.

Charles Freyberg, editorial support.

Corey Lau, support.

David Sands and participants of the Signet Writers Group.

Philip Lindsay, encouragement, patronage.

Tracee Matthews, support, financial assistance.

Jenny Smith, harp rescue, support and financial assistance.

David Spangaro, support.

John Stapleton, editing, support.

Tony Swanston, editing, support.

Cara Macdougall, support.

Tony Zuber, support.

I would like to write a special thanks to all those who wrote letters of support not previously listed, including Ros and Graeme Barnett, Dr Michael Crooks, Deanne Devers, Ben Edwards and Tilley Wilson, Jess and Amber Edwards, Lucinda and Alasdair Edwards, Robert and Vivienne

Edwards , Ann and John Edwards, Clodagh Jones, Julie Kalman and all the staff at Beronia Court. Woy Woy; I would also like to thank Sharon Lierse, Ms Kim Mares, Andrew and Kathleen McMahon, John Moodie, Rosemary Pickstone, Julian Punch, Dr Clair Smith, Jane Swanston, Michelle Warren, Gary and Sandy Watkins, Mal and Bruce Wilkinson, Nina and Stephen Wright and Janette and Brian

www.ingramcontent.com/pod-product-compliance
Lightning Source LLC
Chambersburg PA
CBHW051428290426
44109CB00016B/1468